Gregory Fuller

# True heroes

## Human rights activists change the world



Ernst Klett Verlag
Stuttgart · Leipzig

# Contents

## Before you read this book

*Think about these questions and write down your answers:*

1. *Do you have any personal heroes? If yes, who are they and why are they your heroes? If not, why not?*
2. *Look at the Reading help on pp. 54-55. It will help you to understand and work with this book.*

## Indroduction

In the days before 1945, people never thought much about the term "hero". Great statesmen such as Abraham Lincoln or Otto von Bismarck, or great military strategists such as Alexander the Great, Caesar or Napoleon were often considered "heroes". But after the horrors of World War II, the term did not seem appropriate any more – at least to Europeans, and especially to Germans. The military and political so-called heroes had caused terrible sadness to the world. German history was broken once in 1918 and again in 1945 after the two world wars. Europe and especially Germany became a post-heroic society. It looked as if heroes were not needed any more in democratic and multicultural societies.

Other countries with an unbroken history such as the United States of America had and still have no difficulties with the term "hero". George Washington, Abraham Lincoln, generals such as Dwight D. Eisenhower or Douglas MacArthur, the firefighters of Manhattan who died trying to save people from the burning World Trade Center towers on 11th September, 2001 – for Americans, all these people are true heroes.

This book contains only a few examples of people one could call "heroes". At the end of this book you can think about whether one should still use the term "hero" or not.

---

11 **post-heroic** [ˌpəʊsthɪˈrəʊɪk] nachheroisch • 14 **unbroken** [ʌnˈbrəʊkn] *hier:* unbelastet • 17 **general** [ˈdʒenrl] General, Oberbefehlshaber • 22 **to contain** [kənˈteɪn] beinhalten

## Human rights vocabulary

*These words are often used to talk about human rights:*

to be arrested – verhaftet werden
massacre – Massaker
to be mistreated – misshandelt werden
civil resistance – ziviler Widerstand
non-violence – Gewaltlosigkeit
civil disobedience – ziviler Ungehorsam
courage/courageous – Mut, mutig
oppressed, oppression – unterdrückt, Unterdrückung
to defend oneself – sich verteidigen
outlawed/banned – gesetzwidrig
„ethnic cleansing“ – „ethnische Säuberung“
persecution – Verfolgung
press censorship – Pressezensur
to be executed – hingerichtet werden
racist – rassistisch
free elections – freie Wahlen
reconciliation – Versöhnung
to gain power – an die Macht kommen
regime – (nicht legitime) Regierung
good cause – gute Sache
to go to prison – ins Gefängnis gehen
to renounce violence – der Gewalt entsagen
intellectual – Intellektuelle(r)
to rescue – retten
international outrage – internationaler Aufschrei
injustice – Ungerechtigkeit
to be sentenced to – verurteilt werden zu
to stand up for one's beliefs – Zivilcourage zeigen
to violate human rights – Menschenrechte verletzen

*What does it mean to fight for human rights?*
*Discuss with a partner using the terms above.*

# Gandhi's long Salt March

12th March, 1930, was the beginning of the end of British rule in India. India, it was said, was the crown jewel of the British Empire. A thin little man named Mohandas K. Gandhi started a journey with a few thousand of his followers to the salt fields on the coast. Having the monopoly for the sales of salt in India was seen as the privilege of power. That power was the British Empire.

Gandhi and his followers started their 300 km march from Ahmedabad to the coast where the British had their salt works, in Dharasana. Gandhi and his followers wanted to break the British monopoly on salt. When they reached the salt works, the police were waiting for them.

The peaceful demonstrators were clubbed brutally by the police that served the British rulers. One row of demonstrators after another fell to the ground and were taken off to prison, badly hurt or dying. They did not fight back, they were very disciplined. Gandhi had not been able

**Salt March** ['sɔ:lt mɑ:tʃ] Salzmarsch • 2 **crown jewel** [ˌkraʊn 'dʒu:əl] Kronjuwel • 5 **follower** ['fɒləʊə] Anhänger/-in • 6 **monopoly** [mə'nɒpli] Monopol(stellung) • 7 **privilege** ['prɪvlɪdʒ] Privileg • 13 **to club** [klʌb] (ver-)prügeln • 16 **to be taken off to prison** [ˌteɪkn 'ɒf] ins Gefängnis gebracht werden

to break the British salt monopoly, but he had achieved a much greater victory. His and his followers' civil resistance had broken the moral power of the British Empire.

Mohandas Gandhi was born in Porbandar, India, in 1869. He came from a family of civil servants. Acting in an ethical way – doing the right thing – was very important in Gandhi's family. From an early age, Gandhi learned how important it was to be an honest human being. When he grew up, Gandhi decided to study law in London. After becoming a lawyer he moved to South Africa, in those days part of the great British Empire. In South Africa he was confronted with the early forms of Apartheid. Even rich Indians were not allowed to travel in the first class of trains or stay overnight in good hotels. These were reserved for whites only. In Gandhi's family right and wrong were very important, so the laws in South Africa were terrible for a young man such as Gandhi who believed in democracy. He organized protest marches against discrimination and slowly developed his strategy of peaceful resistance which he called Satyagraha. What people believe, he thought, was more important than what they achieve in life.

In 1897 he was beaten by a white mob in Durban. He felt sorry for the ignorant people who had hurt him and did not take them to court. In 1908 he went to prison for the first time. That did not stop him. He led more and more protest marches against the racist laws of South Africa and gave up his job as a lawyer. Gandhi tried to live the simple life, but it was a very political life. When he returned to India in 1915, he was already famous. Tens of thousands of people came to see him arrive in India by ship. The Indian people who wanted their freedom from Britain called their new leader "Mahatma", Great Soul, and he is known as Mahatma Gandhi to this day.

2 **victory** [ˈvɪktri] Sieg • 2 **resistance** [rɪˈzɪstns] Widerstand • 5 **civil servant** [ˌsɪvl ˈsɜːvnt] (Staats)beamte(r)/ -beamtin • 8 **honest** [ˈɒnɪst] aufrichtig • 20 **Satyagraha** *(Sanskrit)* [səˌtijɑːˈgrɑːhə] • 22 **to beat, beat, beaten** [biːt] (zusammen)schlagen • 24 **to take s.o. to court** [kɔːt] jdn vor Gericht bringen

Gandhi and other political leaders led one peaceful demonstration after another. Gandhi's greatest demonstration was the well-organized march to the salt mines. It was a symbolic march, but the result was not symbolic. The Indian Satyagrahis lost this first great battle to the police, but they gained a great moral victory. In the end, they would win their struggle for freedom.

During World War II Great Britain began to lose its power over the Empire. Britain lost one Southeast Asian country after another to the Japanese army. If it had not been for the United States of America, Britain would have lost the War, too. The Empire's weakness was obvious to the whole world. In 1947 Britain finally gave India its independence.

Gandhi saw his own life as a row of "experiments with truth", as he wrote. He thought about every experience, learned its lessons and gained energy from it. Every new experience helped him to do the right thing the next time.

The next time came in 1948. After independence, Gandhi was not allowed to live the simple country life that he loved. India was split into a mostly Hindu India and a Moslem Pakistan. Terrible riots followed, with thousands and thousands of people being killed by Hindu and Moslem mobs. At the age of 78, on 13th January, 1948, Gandhi began a fast to try to convince people to stop the bloodshed. After five days the political leaders of both countries said they would stop the fighting, and Gandhi broke his fast.

Twelve days later he was shot by a Hindu fanatic who was against Gandhi's programme of peace, tolerance and non-violence. The world was horrified. Gandhi, perhaps, was the greatest human being of the 20th century. His idea of civil disobedience became the central idea of many

**6 to gain a moral victory** [ˌgeɪn ə mɒrl ˈvɪktri] einen moralischen Sieg erringen • **16 to gain energy from sth** [geɪn ˈenədʒi] von etw. inspiriert werden • **22 riot** [ˈraɪət] Ausschreitung • **25 fast** [fɑːst] Hungerstreik • **26 bloodshed** [ˈblʌdʃed] Blutvergießen • **28 to break, broke, broken** [breɪk] *hier:* beenden • **31 non-violence** [ˌnɒnˈvaɪələns] Gewaltfreiheit • **31 perhaps** [pəˈhæps] vielleicht

civil rights movements, such as the American civil rights movement in the 1950s and 1960s. The thin little man was killed in 1948, but his principle of Satyagraha will live on forever.

Nelson Mandela wrote about Gandhi (in the essay *The Sacred Warrior*, TIME Magazine, 3rd January 2000), “Gandhi ... is the archetypical anti-colonial revolutionary. His strategy of non-cooperation, his assertion that we can be dominated only if we cooperate with our dominators, and his non-violent resistance inspired anti-colonial and anti-racist movements internationally in our century.”

## Raoul Wallenberg, Swedish saviour

Between July 1944 and early in 1945, when the Soviet Red Army entered Budapest in Hungary, the Swedish attaché Raoul Wallenberg saved the lives of between 20,000 and 100,000 Jews from the Nazis. How a single human being could do this is one of the great humanist adventures of all time.

Raoul Wallenberg (1912 – ?; pronunciation: ˈvʌlənberi) came from one of the most famous families in Sweden. It is one of the ironies of history that Raoul’s uncles Jacob and Marcus Wallenberg, bankers and industrialists, were doing business with Nazi Germany, while their nephew was saving the lives of thousands of Jews in Budapest at the same time.

Raoul studied to be an architect. While he was working in a Dutch bank in Haifa (Palestine) in the 1930s, he heard the terrible stories of Jewish emigrants from Nazi Germany (1933-45). Their stories of Nazi crimes against Jews in

7 **archetypical anti-colonial revolutionary** [ˌɑːkɪˈtɪpɪkl ˌæntɪkəˈləʊniəl ˌrevlˈuːʃnri] erzantikolonialistischer Revolutionär/-in • 8 **non-cooperation** [ˌnɒnkəʊˌɒpərˈeɪʃn] Verweigerung der Zusammenarbeit • 8 **assertion** [əˈsɜːʃn] Behauptung • 9 **dominator** [ˈdɒmɪneɪtə] Beherrscher/in • **saviour** [ˈseɪvjə] Retter/-in • 15 **Jew** [dʒuː] Jude/Jüdin • 22 **nephew** [ˈnefjuː] Neffe • 26 **Dutch** [dʌtʃ] niederländisch

Germany horrified the sensitive Swede. When Wallenberg had to go on business trips to Nazi Germany before 1939, he learned how German bureaucracy worked. This was to prove extremely important for him a few years later.

In the spring of 1944 Hitler's "Endlösung", the Holocaust or Shoah as it was later called, became known. The American War Refugee Board cooperated with any European embassy that wanted to save the lives of European Jews.

The Swedish embassy in Budapest was especially active. Even the Swedish king did everything he could – successfully. Before Wallenberg arrived in Budapest in July, 1944, the Swedish embassy had issued so-called "Protection Passports" for the Jews. The young and courageous diplomat Per Anger had begun the Protection Passport operation. Another young Swedish diplomat rented buildings from the Red Cross and put up signs over the entrances such as "The Swedish Library" and "The Swedish Research Institute". Jews were brought to the buildings to live there, in relative safety.

But when Wallenberg arrived in Budapest, a true "saviour angel", as he was also called, he put a new dimension to the Swedish rescue operation. He had asked for and received power of attorney from the Swedish king. Wallenberg used these powers to hand out Swedish Protection Passports to the Jews as he wanted to. Officially he was only allowed to hand out 4,500 passports, but he actually handed out many more.

The Nazi terror got worse and worse. Wallenberg had a terrible enemy in Budapest: Adolf Eichmann. In October 1944 only 200,000 Jews were left in Hungary. Eichmann

7 **War Refugee Board** [wɔː ˌrefjʊ'dʒiː ˌbɔːd] US-Regierungsdienststelle, die Opfern der NS-Diktatur weltweit geholfen hatte • 10 **embassy** ['embəsi] Botschaft • 13 **to issue** ['ɪʃuː] ausstellen • 17 **to rent** [rent] mieten • 22 **angel** ['eɪndʒl] Engel • 24 **power of attorney** [ə'tɜːni] Handlungsvollmacht • 25 **to hand out** [hænd 'aʊt] etw. austeilen

wanted to deport them all to the Nazi death camps, so Wallenberg rented more and more buildings in the Pest part of Budapest – 30 buildings in which 15,000 Jews lived. In November 1944 Eichmann organized his first horrible death march: Jews were supposed to walk 200 km to the death camps. But Wallenberg accompanied the march and handed out food, medicine and Protection Passports. When the SS, led by Eichmann, squeezed Jews into the freight cars of waiting trains, Wallenberg was there with his Swedish passports. Wallenberg's driver, who drove him to the station, said after the War, "Then he (Wallenberg) climbed onto the roof of the train and began to hand out passports through the doors that were not yet closed. He ignored the orders of the Germans to climb down. Then the Hungarian Fascists began to shoot at him and told him to go away. He ignored them and handed out passports to all the hands that reached for them. After Wallenberg had given out the last passports, he ordered everyone with a passport to leave the trains and to go over to a car convoy parked nearby and marked with the Swedish colours …" On the way back to the city Wallenberg and Per Anger wrote the names of the rescued people into the passports.

Wallenberg did everything possible for the Jews. He even invited the enemy he hated, Adolf Eichmann, to dinner to find out his weaknesses. After Wallenberg had criticized the Nazi ideology until there was nothing left of

13 **to accompany** [ə'kʌmpəni] begleiten • 16 **to squeeze** [skwi:z] quetschen, zwängen • 16 **freight car** ['freɪt ˌkɑ:] Wagon • 25 **to reach for sth** [ri:tʃ] nach etw. greifen

it, Eichmann admitted that he was right. He is supposed to have said, "I admit that you are right, Herr Wallenberg. I have never believed in National Socialism, but it gave me power and wealth." At the end of the evening he warned Wallenberg, "Accidents can happen, even to neutral diplomats." Shortly after that, a lorry rammed Wallenberg's car, but nobody was hurt.

In the second week of January, 1945, Eichmann planned a massacre in the Jewish Ghetto of Budapest. Thanks to Wallenberg the German army General August Schmidthuber gave a counter-order and didn't go through with the massacre. Wallenberg had warned him that he would see to it that he would be made responsible for the massacre after the War.

After the Red Army entered Budapest in early 1945, any trace of Wallenberg disappears. The Stalinist NKWD, the Secret Police, arrested Wallenberg because they believed he was an American spy. After many, many years the American news magazine *U.S. News and World Report* of 13th May, 1996, confirmed that Wallenberg had worked for the American OSS, the Office of Strategic Services. He had informed the OSS about people trying to separate the alliance between Berlin and Budapest as well as about Soviet army positions. Probably this was the way that Wallenberg received American support for his risky rescue operations.

The Swedish government tried for many years to find out what had happened to Wallenberg. The Soviet government told them that Wallenberg had died of a heart attack in a Soviet prison in 1947. People who were freed from the Soviet work camps, the Gulags, said they had

11 **counter-order** [ˌkaʊntəˈɔːdə] Gegenbefehl • 13 **responsible** [rɪˈspɒsəbl] verantwortlich • 16 **trace** [ˈtreɪs] Spur • 16 **Stalinist NKWD** [ˈstɑːlɪnɪst en keɪ ˈdbljuː diː] Vorläufer des KGB • 17 **to arrest** [əˈrest] verhaften • 18 **spy** [ˈspaɪ] Spion/in • 21 **Office of Strategic Services (OSS)** [ˈɒfɪs əv strəˌtiːdʒɪk ˈsɜːvɪsɪz] Vorläufer der CIA • 23 **alliance** [əˈlaɪəns] Allianz, Bündnis

seen him many years later in several Gulags. To this day it is not known what happened to him after 1945.

Wallenberg and Per Anger received many honours. In 1949 Albert Einstein nominated Wallenberg for the Nobel Peace Prize. In 1953 he was named one of the "Just" in Israel. The United States of America, in 1981, gave him an honorary American citizenship. Sir Winston Churchill and he were the only human beings ever honoured in this way.

In Hungary over 120,000 Jews survived the Nazi persecution. His friend Per Anger said that Wallenberg saved even more than 100,000 Jews from certain death. "I had no choice," Wallenberg said. "I took over the task and I could never return to Stockholm without knowing that I had done everything a man could do to rescue as many Jews as possible."

In the history of humanity Wallenberg's commitment is without parallel. He had done everything humanly possible. Wallenberg risked his life and lost it – but he won the battle against a much stronger enemy.

## Rosa Parks stays seated

Most historians say that the beginning of the modern civil rights movement was on 1st December, 1955, in Montgomery, Alabama. What happened on that day changed the face of the United States of America and inspired civil rights activists throughout the world.

In those days, black and white people in the American South were segregated – separated – in almost every aspect

3 **honour** ['ɒnə] Ehrung • 4 **Nobel Peace Prize** [nəʊˌbel 'piːs ˌpraɪz] Friedensnobelpreis • 5 **the Just** [dʒʌst] die Gerechten • 7 **honorary citizenship** [ˌɒnrəri 'sɪtɪznʃɪp] Ehrenstaatsbürgerschaft • 13 **to take over a task** [teɪk 'əʊvə ə ˌtɑːsk] eine Aufgabe übernehmen • 17 **humanity** [hjuː'mænəti] Menschheit • 17 **commitment** [kə'mɪtmənt] Engagement • 18 **to be without parallel** ['pærəlel] einzigartig sein • 25 **throughout the world** [θrʊˌaʊt ðə 'wɜːld] in der ganzen Welt

of their daily life. These segregation laws were known as "Jim Crow" laws. During World War II, black regiments were separate from white regiments; blacks were allowed to die for their country, but not to mix with whites. In the South black and white children went to different schools. While there were special school buses to take white children to their schools, black children had to walk. Bus and train companies had separate seat sections for white and black people. In Montgomery, Alabama, the first four rows of seats in public buses were reserved for white people. The seats for the black people, called "colored", were in the back of the bus, but not fixed places. Black people could also sit in the middle sections until the white section was full. Then they had to move to seats in the back, or to stand or, if the bus was full, to leave the bus. Black people were not allowed to sit across from white people, and black people had to pay their fare at the bus driver's, then leave the bus and get on in the back.

Coming home from her job as a tailor's assistant in a department store, 42-year-old Rosa Parks (1913 to 2005) was tired. She sat down in the middle section of a public bus. When more white passengers got on, the white bus driver told four black passengers to go to the back of the bus. Three did as he said, but Rosa Parks wouldn't move. In her autobiography *My story* she wrote: "People always said that I didn't give up my seat because I was tired, but that isn't true ... No, the only tired I was, was tired of giving in."

The bus driver called the police and Rosa Parks was arrested.

---

2 **Jim Crow laws** [dʒɪm ˈkrəʊ lɔːz] Gesetze (von 1876 bis 1965) wodurch Schwarze getrennte öffentliche Einrichtungen benutzen mussten • 3 **regiment** [ˈredʒɪmənt] Regiment • 8 **section** [ˈsekʃn] Abteil, Bereich • 12 **fixed** [fɪkst] fest • 19 **tailor** [ˈteɪlə] Schneider/-in • 27 **to give in** [gɪv ˈɪn] nachgeben

Two friends, one of them white, paid the 100 Dollars bail, so Rosa Parks could go home until her trial. She was later sentenced to a fine of 14 Dollars, but she did not accept the verdict. In 1956 the United States Supreme Court outlawed segregation on buses in the states.

During this time, on 5th December, 1955, a young minister named Dr. Martin Luther King, Jr., spoke in a Montgomery church. "There comes a time that people get tired," he said. "We are here this evening to say to those who have mistreated us for so long that we are tired, tired of being segregated and humiliated, tired of being kicked about by the brutal feet of oppression." As Gandhi had once done, Dr. King told his followers to stay peaceful: "We must meet violence with non-violence." The bus boycott, which had already started, continued for altogether 381 days and

2 **bail** [beɪl] Kaution • 2 **trial** ['traɪəl] Gerichtsverfahren, Prozess • 3 **to sentence** ['sentəns] verurteilen • 3 **fine** [faɪn] Geldstrafe • 4 **verdict** ['vɜːdɪkt] Urteil • 4 **Supreme Court** [suːˌpriːm 'kɔːt] Oberstes Bundesgericht • 5 **to outlaw** ['aʊtlɔː] *hier:* verbieten • 10 **to mistreat so** [mɪs'triːt] misshandeln • 11 **to humiliate** [hjuː'mɪlieɪt] erniedrigen • 12 **oppression** [ə'preʃn] Unterdrückung

made Dr. King a leader of the civil rights movement, and little Rosa Parks became a symbol for the civil rights of all oppressed people worldwide.

Rosa Parks lost her job at the department store, and later she and her husband, a barber, who also lost his job, moved to Detroit, Michigan.

When she died at 92 in 2005, she had received many honours. Her casket could be visited in the United States Capitol in Washington for two days, an honour usually reserved for Presidents of the United States. Americans, black and white, could pay their respects to this little woman whose courage changed the lives of millions.

## Nelson Mandela forgives his enemies

In 1990, after 27 long years in prison, Nelson Mandela was a free man. He was 72 years old. His spirit was not broken by those terrible years, and he was not full of hate. As a famous international figure and lifelong activist in the political party called the (South) African National Congress, the ANC, he immediately supported reconciliation and negotiation with the white Apartheid regime of South Africa. In those days, blacks and whites were separate in all ways of life, and the black majority was brutally oppressed by the white minority – about 11% of the population. Mandela asked his followers to stay peaceful.

For achieving reconciliation and a peaceful transition to democracy, Mandela and the South African President de Klerk together received the Nobel Peace Prize in 1993.

5 **husband** ['hʌzbənd] Ehemann • 8 **casket** ['kɑ:skɪt] Sarg • 11 **to pay one's respects** [ˌpeɪ wʌnz rɪ'spekts] jmdm. die letzte Ehre erweisen • **to forgive** [fə'gɪv] vergeben • 18 **immediately** [ɪ'mi:diətli] sofort • 19 **reconciliation** [ˌreknsɪli'eɪʃn] Aussöhnung • 19 **negotiation** [ˌnegəʊʃi'eɪʃn] Verhandlung • 21 **majority** [mə'dʒɒrəti] Mehrheit • 25 **transition** [træn'zɪʃn] Übergang

Born Rolihlahla Mandela (Xhosa pronunciation: xo'lilʌlʌ mʌn'deɪlʌ) in Transkei, South Africa, in 1918, he was named "Nelson" by his teacher at school. It sounded more British. "Rolihlahla" means "troublemaker", and Mandela's real name was prophetic. He really did become a troublemaker for the racist Apartheid regime, but much later in life.

He was an intelligent boy and, as Gandhi had done, he studied law to become a lawyer. While studying law in Johannesburg in 1942, he joined the ANC. There was little time for him to practice law because he organized resistance to discriminatory laws. The Transvaal Law Society wanted to have him removed as a lawyer, but an honest judge wouldn't allow this, saying that Mandela was really trying to help South Africa's black citizens.

During the 1950s, Mandela was banned, arrested and put in jail, then set free again, always watched closely by the secret police. In 1960, many black South Africans were shot by the police during a demonstration. It became known as the Sharpeville Massacre. The ANC was outlawed. Because of this, the ANC had to change their strategy.

In those years, members of the ANC had very different opinions of how they could overcome Apartheid. Many wanted to follow a slow way to freedom, but many others preferred using violence, now that they were illegal. The white minority, it had become clear, would never give up

2 **Xhosa** ['kɔ:sə] eine Bantusprache • 9 **troublemaker** ['trʌblˌmeɪkə] Unruhestifter, Querulant • 18 **to practice law** [ˌpræktɪs 'lɔ:] den Anwaltsberuf ausüben • 19 **discriminatory** [dɪ'skrɪmɪnətri] diskriminierend • 20 **to remove so** [rɪ'mu:v] jmdn. entlassen • 23 **to ban so** [bæn] jdn. ausschließen

its power. In 1961 Mandela became the leader of the Armed Wing of the ANC, Umkhonto we Sizwe, meaning *Spear of the Nation*. Mandela coordinated sabotage against the army and government – but in a way that nobody would be injured. Much later in life Mandela said that his sabotage acts also violated human rights. But in those years he saw no other way, after decades of oppression by the racist white Apartheid regime.

For 17 months Mandela hid from the police. Finally, they caught him in August, 1962. At his trial, he said, "During my lifetime I have dedicated myself to the struggle of the African people. I have fought against white domination, and I have fought black domination. I have cherished the ideal of a democratic and free society in which all persons live together in harmony and with equal opportunities. It is an ideal which I hope to live for and to achieve. But if needs be, it is an ideal for which I am prepared to die." He was sentenced to five years in prison.

Five years wasn't enough for the Apartheid regime. While in prison, Mandela was again put on trial in 1964, and it wasn't clear whether he would have to stay in prison for life or whether he would be executed by the Apartheid regime. Finally, he received a sentence of life imprisonment.

Mandela was taken to Robben Island, 7 km off the coast near Cape Town, where he stayed for the next 18 of his 27 years in prison. As a black political prisoner, he was a D-group prisoner, the lowest group. He was allowed one visitor and one letter every six months. He became more and more famous as one of the most important political prisoners in the world. More and more pressure was brought on the South African government to free Nelson

**1 armed** [ɑ:md] bewaffnet • **2 spear** [spɪə] Speer • **6 to violate** ['vaɪəleɪt] verletzen • **11 to dedicate oneself to sth** ['dedɪkeɪt] sich etw. widmen • **11 struggle** ['stʌgl] Kampf • **12 domination** [ˌdɒmɪ'neɪʃn] (Vor)Herrschaft • **13 to cherish sth** ['tʃerɪʃ] etw. wertschätzen • **16 if needs be** [ɪf 'ni:dz bi:] hier: wenn es sein muss • **17 prepared** [prɪ'peəd] bereit sein • **22 to execute so** ['eksɪkju:t] jdn. hinrichten

Mandela and his friends – not only by many governments, but also by rock stars: Free Nelson Mandela!

Mandela was becoming a great man. Every prisoner had great respect for him, and he did everything he could to help the other prisoners. His influence on the young black activist prisoners became so great that in 1982 he was taken to a different prison. In 1985 the South African President Botha made Mandela an offer: If he would renounce violence, he would be freed. Mandela turned the offer down. He sent his message through his daughter Zindzi, "What freedom am I being offered while the organization of the people remains banned? Only free men can negotiate. A prisoner cannot enter into contracts."

President Botha became very ill in 1989, and Frederick Willem de Klerk became President. The international pressure by many countries and by the United Nations had now become so great that President de Klerk did the only thing sensible: he lifted the ban on the ANC and other anti-Apartheid organizations, and he released Nelson Mandela after 27 years in prison, on 11th February, 1990.

9 **to renounce** [rɪ'naʊns] abschwören, sich abwenden von • 9 **to turn sth down** [tɜːn 'daʊn] etw. abweisen • 12 **to remain** [rə'meɪn] bleiben • 18 **sensible** ['sensɪbl] vernünftig • 19 **to release** [rɪ'liːs] freilassen

ANC members and anti-Apartheid people around the world went wild with joy. Shortly after he was released, Mandela and the ANC said they would not use violence any longer. The days of the Apartheid regime were coming to an end. In 1991, at the first national conference of the ANC inside South Africa after being banned for 30 years, Nelson Mandela became president of the ANC. He continued his negotiations with President de Klerk, and de Klerk realized that he would be the last white President of South Africa. The Nobel Peace Prize in 1993 encouraged both parties to find a peaceful transition from Apartheid to democracy, and they did.

The ANC became a political party and won 62% of the votes in the first free national elections in the Republic of South Africa. Nelson Mandela became the first democratically elected President of South Africa in 1994, and he stayed President until 1999.

During the years as President he continued to bring whites and blacks in South Africa together. He was one of the most respected leaders in the world. He received over fifty honours and honorary doctorates from universities all over the world.

He had become a living legend, a hero of the 20th century. In his autobiography *Long walk to freedom*, 1994, he wrote, "I knew as well as I knew anything that the oppressor must be liberated just as surely as the oppressed. A man who takes away another man's freedom is a prisoner of hatred ... I am not truly free if I am taking away someone else's freedom, just as surely as I am not free if my freedom is taken from me. The oppressed and the oppressor alike are robbed of their humanity."

10 **to encourage so to do sth** [ɪn'kʌrɪdʒ] jmdn. ermuntern, etw. zu tun • 21 **honorary doctorate** ['ɒnrəri 'dɒktrət] Ehrendoktorwürde/-titel • 26 **to liberate** ['lɪbreɪt] befreien • 27 **hatred** ['heɪtrɪd] Hass • 28 **truly** ['tru:li] wahrhaftig • 30 **alike** [ə'laɪk] gleichermaßen • 31 **to rob** [rɒb] (be)rauben • 31 **humanity** [hju:'mænəti] *hier:* Menschlichkeit, Würde

## Aung San Suu Kyi and the generals

Burma is a strange country. Since 1962 it has been ruled by a military junta, by a group of generals. In 1989 they decided to call the country "Myanmar". Once Burma used to be called The Jewel of Asia or The Golden Country. "It is hard to ruin a state that two generations ago was considered potentially one of the richest in Asia," David Steinberg said, Professor at Georgetown University, Washington, D.C. "But the military government actually managed to do it." The World Report of Economic Freedom puts Burma, out of 123 states, at the very end, at 123rd place. The military junta of generals spends 0.15% of its annual budget on education, and 40% of the population live below the poverty level. The only productive area is drugs. The main amount of opium for the world markets comes from Afghanistan, Pakistan and the Golden Triangle.

"On the road to Mandalay/Down where elephants play" Rudyard Kipling, a British author, once wrote about Burma when it was still a British colony, but British colonialism was hard on Burma. Today Burma's situation is even worse, and elephants do not play there any more. In 2009 the International Human Rights Clinic at Harvard Law School (Cambridge, Massachusetts) reported systematic killings, torture, rape and "epidemic levels" of forced labor, a million people homeless and thousands and thousands of child soldiers, some of them only 11 years old. Thousands of opposition members are in prison or were murdered by the army. When Cyclone Nargis destroyed much of the Burmese Irrawaddy Delta in 2008, the generals did not want to let any foreign aid into the country for many weeks. As a result of this, thousands of Burmese died

1 **to rule** [ruːl] regieren • 2 **junta** [ˈdʒʌntə] Junta (Militär bildet den machthabenden Teil der Staatsregierung) • 9 **economic** [ˌiːkəˈnɒmɪk] Wirtschafts- • 11 **annual budget** [ˈænjʊəl ˌbʌdʒɪt] Jahresetat • 15 **Golden Triangle** [ˈtraɪæŋgl] opiumreiche Region Südostasiens • 23 **torture** [ˈtɔːtʃə] Folter • 23 **rape** [reɪp] Vergewaltigung • 23 **forced labor** [fɔːst ˈleɪbə] Zwangsarbeit • 27 **cyclone** [ˈsaɪkləʊn] Zyklon • 29 **aid** [eɪd] Hilfe

unnecessarily. The United States of America has placed an economic investment embargo on the country and only a few countries such as China still do business with the generals. The United Nations can do nothing because two Security Council members, Russia and China, do not want to act against Burma. In August 2009, American President Barack Obama asked the generals to free all political prisoners in Burma. For years, different generals have led the country, but the army held together, and there was always a new general to become the leading figure. Burma has a human rights record hardly better than North Korea, the most brutal regime in the world today.

There is widespread Burmese and international opposition to the generals. Every few years, mass protests are heard and seen, and then they are heard no more. "We speak, we die," as Burmese political opponents of the generals have quietly said.

But there is one person in Burma who, over the decades, has been courageous enough to speak out against the junta again and again, calling for democracy. Out of respect the Burmese call her *The Lady*, or *Daw*, which means *aunt*. Her name is Aung San Suu Kyi (pronunciation: ʌʊn ˌsʌnsu: ˈtʃi:).

**1 to place (on)** [pleɪs] verhängen • **2 investment embargo** [ɪnˈvestmənt ɪmˈbɑ:gəʊ] Investitionsembargo • **5 Security Council** [sɪˈkjʊərəti ˌkaʊnsl] (UN-) Sicherheitsrat • **16 opponent** [əˈpəʊnənt] Gegner/in • **19 over the decades** [ˌəʊvə ðə ˈdekeɪdz] über die Jahrzehnte hinweg • **21 courageous** [kəˈreɪdʒəs] mutig • **26 Daw** [daʊ]

Born in 1945 in Rangoon, the capital of Burma, Suu Kyi studied philosophy, politics and economics at Oxford and continued her studies in New York. She married a British Tibetologist and has two sons. She has lived in the UK, the US, Bhutan and Japan. When she was back in Rangoon in 1988 because her mother was dying, mass protests against the generals broke out. In the same year, the Burmese National League for Democracy (NLD) was formed with Suu Kyi as secretary general. In her first public speech in August 1988, she called for democracy. During the mass protests, thousands of people were killed by the army, but Suu Kyi gave speeches throughout the country.

One day in 1989, when she was in the Irrawaddy Delta, she was stopped by soldiers who aimed their guns at her. She courageously walked towards the soldiers, and they did not shoot. Instead, she was placed under house arrest, without any trial. Her husband Michael flew into Rangoon and found her on her third day of hunger strike because students were arrested in her home and taken to prison. When good treatment of the students was promised, Suu Kyi ended her hunger strike – the first of many hunger strikes.

Her voice was heard more and more inside and outside Burma, and she became the Burmese voice of freedom. National elections were held in 1990 in Burma, and to the surprise of the generals, Suu Kyi's NLD won 82% of the vote! Suu Kyi was to become president of Burma, but the generals ignored the results of the elections. They stayed in power, even though there was an international protest against them. In July 1991 the European Parliament awarded Suu Kyi the Sakharov Prize for human rights, and

4 **Tibetologist** [ˌtɪbət'ɔːlɪdʒɪst] Tibetologe/Tibetologin • 8 **National League for Democracy** [liːg] politische Oppositionspartei gegen die Militärjunta • 8 **to form** [fɔːm] gründen • 14 **to aim** [eɪm] auf jmdn. richten • 16 **to place sb under house arrest** [pleɪs ˌʌndə 'haʊs əˌrest] jmdn. unter Hausarrest stellen • 31 **to award** [ə'wɔːd] verleihen, ehren mit • 31 **Sakharov Prize** ['sækərɒf praɪz] Preis für Aktionen, die zur Verteidigung der Menschenrechte dienen

in October of the same year she was awarded the Nobel Peace Prize. Her sons Alexander and Kim went to Oslo to accept the prize. Suu Kyi had rejected various offers by the generals to leave the country and return again, but she did not believe them. She did not even dare to leave the country in 1999, when her husband was dying of cancer in London.

Over the next years, Suu Kyi was in and out of prison and mostly under house arrest. Of the last 20 years, she spent 14 in prison or under house arrest.

She was released in 2002 after the United Nations helped to create a dialogue between her and the junta. When she was travelling around Burma in 2003, a mob paid by the government attacked her convoy, killing many of Suu Kyi's supporters, known as the Depayin Massacre. Suu Kyi was saved by her driver who fled the scene, but later she was arrested again, sent to prison and then forced under house arrest again. In 2007, solidarity demonstrations were held in 12 cities around the world, and there were Burmese mass protests against the generals' rule, led by Buddhist monks. Soon enough, the generals ordered the army to shoot the demonstrators, and an unknown number of people were murdered and put into prison. In 2008 Suu Kyi's house arrest was extended for another year. When in 2009 a religious American man swam across the lake near her house to warn her, he said, that her life was in danger, Suu Kyi was accused of violating the trespass act (not allowing her to talk to foreigners). Her house arrest was extended for another 18 months. By then, she had become the Gandhi of Burma, who was a respected international figure as Nelson Mandela was.

Aung San Suu Kyi always believed in Gandhi's principles of non-violence and civil disobedience. In *The Voice of*

3 **to reject** [rɪˈdʒekt] ablehnen • 5 **to dare to do sth** [deə] wagen etw. zu tun • 15 **supporter** [səˈpɔːtə] Anhänger/in • 21 **monk** [mʌŋk] Mönch • 24 **to extend (for)** [ɪkˈstend] verlängern (um) • 27 **to accuse sb of doing sth** [əˈkjuːz] beschuldigen • 27 **trespass act** [ˈtrespəs ækt] Zutrittsverbot

*Hope* she wrote: "I do not believe in an armed struggle because it will perpetuate the tradition that he who is best at wielding arms, wields power. That will not help democracy." She also wrote:

"Non-violence is a positive action. You have to work for whatever you want. ... It just means that the methods you use are not violent ones. Some people think that non-violence is passiveness. It's not so. I know it is the slower way, and I understand why our young people feel that it will not work. But I cannot encourage that kind of attitude. Because if I do, we will be perpetuating the cycle of violence that will never come to an end." When she was asked if she was never afraid, she answered, "I am afraid. I am afraid of doing the wrong thing that might bring harm to others."

When Suu Kyi was told she was even called "Burma's Saint Joan", she answered, "Good heavens, I hope not."

When Suu Kyi was awarded the Amnesty International Ambassador of Conscience Award in 2009, the Secretary General of Amnesty International, Irene Khan, called Suu Kyi "a symbol of hope and undying defence of human rights, not only to the people of Myanmar but to people around the world."

## Ken Saro-Wiwa and the oil industry

On 21st May, 1994, four Nigerian chiefs from the Ogoni tribe were brutally murdered. To this day, the murders have not been solved. Although he was not allowed to enter Ogoniland on the day of the murders, Ken Saro-Wiwa and

2 **to perpetuate** [pəˈpetʃʊeɪt] fortbestehen lassen • 3 **to wield** [wiːld] schwingen (Waffen); ausüben (Macht) • 11 **attitude** [ˈætɪtjuːd] Einstellung • 11 **cycle** [ˈsaɪkl] *hier:* Spirale • 14 **harm** [hɑːm] Leiden • 17 **Saint Joan** [snt ˈdʒəʊn] Heilige Johanna • 17 **Good heavens** [gʊd ˈhevnz] Um Himmels Willen! • 19 **ambassador** [æmˈbæsədə] Botschafter/in • 19 **conscience** [ˈkɒnʃns] Gewissen • 21 **undying defence** [ʌnˈdaɪɪŋ dɪˈfens] nie endende Verteidigung • **Saro-Wiwa** [ˌsærəʊ ˈviːvə] • 24 **chief** [tʃiːf] Häuptling

eight other Ogoni men were immediately arrested because he was accused of the murder of the four chiefs. But one of Saro-Wiwa's principles was non-violence.

To understand why the four chiefs were murdered, you have to go back a few years and look at Nigerian history. You also have to understand one thing: modern Nigeria, a large and potentially rich country in West Africa, means oil. Nigeria was and still is the largest oil export country in Africa. About 85% of the state revenue comes from oil. It is found offshore and in the Niger Delta which is where the Ogoni tribe lives.

The last fifty years of Nigerian history was a strange mix of democracy, then dictatorship, then democracy ("Second Republic"), then dictatorship etc. In 1995 Sani Abacha became dictator. It was one of the bloodiest dictatorships in Nigerian history. Nigeria is now in its Fourth Republic. A former military dictator, Olusegun Obasanjo, became the first president of this Fourth Republic in 1999.

The first oil company to drill for oil in the Niger Delta in the 1950s was Royal Dutch Shell. More and more companies began to drill for oil there. The Nigerian dictators were helpful towards the oil companies because they profited from them. The dictatorships in Nigerian history were, of course, completely corrupt. They were only interested in staying in power and profiting from the oil money. Millions and millions and millions were made by the large oil companies, and millions of dollars went into the pockets of the dictators. The dictators were not interested in ecology and they did not care about the tribe that lived in the Niger Delta, the Ogoni.

The Ogoni are fishermen and farmers. The pipelines that went through their land and the oil spills from oil

9 **revenue** ['revnju:] Einkommen • 10 **offshore** [ɒf'ʃɔ:] vor der Küste • 17 **former** ['fɔ:mə] ehemalig • 19 **to drill (for)** [drɪl] bohren • 23 **to profit** ['prɒfɪt] profitieren, Gewinn machen • 29 **ecology** [i:'kɒlədʒi] Ökologie, *hier:* Umwelt(schutz) • 32 **oil spill** ['ɔɪl spɪl] Ölteppich

drilling, and the oil in the sea, destroyed their way of life. For decades, oil waste was simply dumped on Ogoni land. The dictators did not want to introduce strict environmental regulations for the oil companies. The environmental damage in the Niger Delta area was and still is an environmental catastrophe for the fishermen and farmers there. They began to get politically organized. One of the leading figures in the Ogoni struggle to clean up the environmental damage was Ken Saro-Wiwa.

Kenule „Ken“ Beeson Saro-Wiwa was born in 1941 in the Niger Delta. He was a member of the Ogoni tribe. He was a very good student and studied English at Government College Umuahia and finished his studies at the University of Ibadan. He worked as businessman and in real estate, and he also became a television producer. His satirical TV series, *Basi & Company*, is said to be the most watched TV soap in Africa. In the early 1970s Saro-Wiwa served as a Regional Commissioner for Education in a democratic government, but was soon dismissed for his support of the Ogoni cause against Shell. Saro-Wiwa's talents did not end there. He became a famous writer, too. His best-known novel is *Sozaboy: A Novel in Rotten English*, 1985. *Sozaboy* means "soldier boy". The novel is written in "Pidgin English", which is spoken in West Africa and in the Pacific and tells the story of a young man

**2 oil waste** [ˈɔɪl weɪst] Ölabfälle • **5 damage** [ˈdæmɪdʒ] Schaden • **20 real-estate** [ˈrɪəl ɪˌsteɪt] Immobilien • **22 television producer** [ˌtelɪvɪʒn prəˈdjuːsə] Fernsehproduzent/in • **26 commissioner** [kəˈmɪʃnə] Beauftragte/r • **27 to dismiss** [dɪˈsmɪs] entlassen

during the Nigerian Civil War of 1967-1970. Saro-Wiwa was also a journalist who realized more and more what was happening to the Ogoni people. He stopped writing in 1987 and became politically active in 1987 to help the new dictator create a transition to democracy. Soon Saro-Wiwa resigned because he was sure that the dictator, Ibrahim Babangida, did not want to give up political power. Saro-Wiwa was, unfortunately, right. Babangida annulled the Nigerian elections and stayed in power himself.

More and more, Saro-Wiwa did everything possible for human rights and the environmental cause of the Niger Delta. It was impossible to separate the two. He and other Ogoni founded the Movement for the Survival of the Ogoni people (MOSOP) in 1990. Saro-Wiwa spent his time writing and organizing MOSOP. In *Nigeria, The Brink of Disaster* and *Genocide in Nigeria* (1992) Saro-Wiwa strongly criticized corruption in Nigeria as well as Shell and British Petroleum (BP) for the environmental damage they had caused in the Niger Delta. From 1993 to 1995, Saro-Wiwa became Vice-President of Unrepresented Nations and Peoples (UNPO), an international, non-violent organization of which MOSOP is a member. The members of UNPO are minorities and indigenous peoples who have come together to fight non-violently for their rights and their traditional culture and to preserve their natural environment. In January 1993 the largest peaceful demonstration in history took place. Saro-Wiwa and other leaders of MOSOP mobilized 300,000 Ogoni – more than half the Ogoni population – to protest against Shell and to demand compensation for the environmental damage that the company had caused.

6 **to resign** [rɪ'zaɪn] aufgeben, zurücktreten • 8 **to annul** [ə'nʌl] für ungültig erklären • 13 **survival** [sə'vaɪvl] Überleben, Erhaltung • 16 **brink (of)** [brɪŋk] kurz vor etw. stehen • 16 **genocide** ['dʒenəsaɪd] Genozid, Völkermord • 20 **unrepresented** [ˌʌnreprɪ'zentɪd] nicht vertreten • 25 **to preserve** [prɪ'zɜ:v] bewahren • 30 **to demand** [dɪ'mɑ:nd] fordern • 30 **compensation** [ˌkɒmpən'seɪʃn] Entschädigung

Ken Saro-Wiwa and other MOSOP leaders were living dangerously. They were in the way of business. Babangida needed a reason to stop Saro-Wiwa who was becoming famous throughout the world. When the four conservative Ogoni chiefs, who did not agree with MOSOP, were murdered on 21st May, 1994, the dictator had a reason for putting Saro-Wiwa and eight other MOSOP leaders in prison.

The men were known as the "Ogoni Nine". They were put on trial which was a "show trial", criticized by many human rights organizations. The dictator brought in witnesses who said the Ogoni Nine had taken part in the murders of the four chiefs. Saro-Wiwa and the other MOSOP leaders denied having anything to do with the murders. Later, the witnesses admitted that they had received money from the government as well as job promises with Shell. In a letter from prison, Saro-Wiwa wrote, "The most important thing for me is that I've used my talents as a writer to enable the Ogoni people to confront their tormentors. I was not able to do it as a politician or a businessman. My writing did it. And it sure makes me feel good! I'm mentally prepared for the worst, but hopeful for the best. I think I have a moral victory."

It was his only victory. Then another dictator took power in Nigeria. The American President, Bill Clinton, asked General Sani Abacha in a phone call to spare Saro-Wiwa's life, but after over a year in prison, the Ogoni Nine were sentenced to death by hanging. On 10th November, 1995, Ken Saro-Wiwa and the other eight Ogoni were hanged by the army. The last to be hanged, Saro-Wiwa had to watch the hanging of his eight friends. He was buried in an unmarked grave. There was immediate international outrage, and Nigeria was no longer allowed to be a

11 **witness** ['witnəs] Zeuge, Zeugin • 14 **to deny** [dɪ'naɪ] zurückweisen • 18 **to enable** [ɪ'neɪbl] etw. ermöglichen • 19 **to confront** [kən'frʌnt] ins Auge sehen • 19 **tormentor** [tɔː'mentə] Peiniger/-in • 26 **to spare** [speə] verschonen • 28 **by hanging** ['hæŋɪŋ] durch den Strang • 31 **to bury** ['beri] begraben • 32 **unmarked grave** [ʌn'mɑːkt greɪv] namenloses Grab • 33 **outrage** ['aʊtreɪdʒ] Empörung

member of the Commonwealth of Nations. The reaction to the hangings by Royal Dutch Shell was – silence.

In 2009, Shell agreed to pay 11.2 million euros to the families of six Nigerian activists hanged in 1995. At the same time, Shell clearly stated that the company had nothing to do with the terrible hangings.

The struggle goes on. Hundreds of human rights activists and environmentalists took over from Ken Saro-Wiwa. An activist, Nnimmo Bassey, said, "Oil has been the destruction of the Nigerian economy. It destroys the relation between the people and the state."

## Julia 'Butterfly' Hill saves a redwood forest

"Love in action has the answer", said Julia Hill who gave herself the name 'Butterfly'. When she was six or seven years old, a butterfly landed on her and stayed there for a few hours while Hill was hiking in the Pennsylvania mountains. Butterflies kept coming to land on her – sometimes in reality and sometimes in Hill's visions.

It is said that a butterfly can create a storm on the other side of the globe. Julia 'Butterfly' Hill did nothing less when she climbed a giant redwood tree in northern California on 10th December, 1997. She called the tree that was over a thousand years old 'Luna', or *Moon*.

Julia Hill could find no other way to protest the felling of the remaining natural forests of North America. Her opponent was the Pacific Lumber Company MAXXAM.

In North America less than three per cent of the very old redwood trees are left standing. Some of those trees are 1,500 years old. Some of the trees are protected, for

10 **destruction** [dɪ'strʌkʃn] Zerstörung • 11 **relation** [rɪ'leɪʃn] Beziehung • **Julia Hill** [ˌdʒuːliə 'hɪl] • **butterfly** ['bʌtəflaɪ] Schmetterling • **redwood** ['redwʊd] Mammutbaum • 24 **remaining** [rɪ'meɪnɪŋ] verbleibend • 25 **lumber** ['lʌmbə] Nutzholz • 28 **to be protected** [prə'tektɪd] *hier:* unter Naturschutz stehen

instance in Sequoia National Park, but many are not protected. Without the redwoods a very special ecology could not exist. The redwood ecosystem gave the Native Americans food to eat. Today, however, large areas of the American Pacific coast are being cleared of old trees. The beautiful redwood can be used for yachts, for floors in houses and for car dashboard decoration.

"I gave my word to this tree and to all the people that my feet would not touch the ground until I had done everything in my power to make the world aware of this problem and to stop the destruction," Hill said. She took part in a demonstration protesting the use of pepper spray by local police. This brought her into contact with a group of environmentalists who were doing a "tree-sit". They needed volunteers, and Julia learned how to climb trees. What had begun as a protest soon turned out to be a gigantic action that the national and international press wrote about and which endangered Hill's life.

At the age of 23, she climbed a redwood and made a home for herself on a six foot by eight foot platform, at about 55m from the ground. It was 10th December, 1997, and she stayed up there until 19th December, 1999, for 738 days, or a bit more than for two years. She did not come down from her platform once. The longer she stayed up on her platform, the more famous she became. People she did not know wrote her encouraging letters. School classes began environmental actions, taking Hill as a model for their protests. Up there on her tree platform Hill wrote about 100 letters a week and telephoned six to eight hours a day, gave interviews and encouraged high school and college students with their own environmental causes.

**1 for instance** [fə 'ɪnstəns] zum Beispiel • **2 ecology** [iː'kɒlədʒi] *hier:* ökologische Nische • **5 to clear an area of trees** [klɪə] die Bäume in einem Gebiet fällen • **7 dashboard** ['dæʃbɔːd] Amaturenbrett • **9 to touch** [tʌtʃ] berühren • **10 to make sb aware** [ə'weə] jdn. aufmerksam machen • **14 environmentalist** [ɪnˌvaɪrən'mentlɪst] Umweltschützer/-in • **14 tree-sit** ['triːsɪt] Baumbesetzung • **17 gigantic** [dʒaɪ'gæntɪk] gigantisch • **23 a bit** [bɪt] ein bisschen • **30 to encourage** [ɪn'kʌrɪdʒ] ermutigen

Often enough there was no chance to sleep. The strong Pacific wind blew in the trees. Hill survived the strongest Pacific storm in northern California by imitating her tree. The tree bent in the wind, so as not to break. Instead of holding on to her tree, Hill sat up freely on her little platform and moved her arms with the wind and sang and laughed. But in fact, nature was not her greatest problem.

The MAXXAM company tried for ten days to starve Hill by cutting the cables that brought food and drink to her up on the platform. The company let a horn blow for 24 hours. MAXXAM sent a helicopter to hover right above Hill's head to make her leave the platform. Hill did not give in.

In the end, MAXXAM was forced to give up. Julia Hill and MAXXAM signed an agreement which stated that Hill's tree Luna and an area of three acres around it would not be touched by the lumber company.

2 **to blow, blew, blown** [bləʊ] wehen • 4 **to bend, bent, bent** [bend] sich biegen, neigen • 8 **to starve** [stɑːv] aushungern • 10 **to blow a horn** [bləʊ‿ə ˈhɔːn] Signal ertönen lassen, Hupgeräusche machen • 11 **to hover** [ˈhʌvə] *hier:* kreisen • 13 **to give in** [ɡɪv ˈɪn] nachgeben • 15 **agreement** [əˈɡriːmənt] Vertrag, Vereinbarung • 16 **acre** [ˈeɪkə] Morgen (ca. 4050 m²)

After 738 days Hill climbed down from her tree. "I collapsed and began to cry," Hill admitted. "But my heart sings for happiness." She had become a new human being after having lived so close to nature and to 'her' tree. "And how am I going to handle losing the best friend I've ever had in my life?" she said about Luna.

Julia Hill was born in 1974 in Fayetteville, Arkansas. As a girl, she was not interested in the environment. But in 1996 she was nearly killed in a car accident, and this changed her life and the way she thought. "Almost a year later I was able to walk and talk and be normal again. At that time I decided everything I had taken for granted had been almost taken away from me, and that I had to start focussing my attention and my life on the real and important things." When she joined some friends on a hiking tour through California, her life was about to change.

"I first saw redwoods in July of '97. I found out in August that they were being destroyed. That's when my passion was sparked. I had planned on going around the world, but when I found out what was happening to the forests I knew I couldn't leave because my inaction would be as much a part of the destruction as the actions of Pacific Lumber MAXXAM. So I sold my belongings, bought a backpack, a good tent and a good camping stove and came out west." The "tree-sit" helped her to find the way.

Hill and her friends founded the Circle of Life Foundation. Hill writes a lot and is a popular public speaker. She is active in many environmental causes. On 17th July, 2002, she was arrested in Quito, Ecuador because she and many other people protested against the North American Occidental Petroleum company which was laying a pipeline. It endangered many towns and villages.

12 **to take sth for granted** [ˈgrɑːntɪd] etw. für selbstverständlich halten • 18 **passion** [ˈpæʃn] Leidenschaft • 19 **to spark** [spɑːk] entfachen • 21 **inaction** [ɪnˈækʃn] Untätigkeit • 23 **belongings** [bɪˈlɒŋɪŋz] Hab und Gut • 24 **backpack** [ˈbækpæk] Rucksack • 24 **camping stove** [ˈkæmpɪŋ stəʊv] Kocher • 26 **circle** [ˈsɜːkl] Kreis • 27 **foundation** [faʊnˈdeɪʃn] Stiftung • 32 **to endanger** [ɪnˈdeɪndʒə] bedrohen, gefährden

"When I was in that tree I learned beyond the shadow of a doubt that every single moment of every day there's a choice, and every single choice affects the world, whether we see it or not." Hill acts according to Gandhi's Satyagraha. "Every time we allow an injustice to happen without speaking out, without acting out, another muscle is gone and another person or another species will pay the price." She calls money that is used to save the environment "green energy". "I will give anything in my life to make the world a better place."

## Hu Jia challenges the Communist Party

In a blog article from 2007, Hu Jia (pronunciation: hu: ˈdʒɑ:; in China and Japan, the last name is written first) stated about China, "Everyone should know that the country that is about to host the Olympics is one without democratic elections, freedom of religion, independent courts or independent unions. ... It is a nation that violates human rights standards and human dignity, and is not ready to fulfil its international obligations."

To understand how a little man like Hu could speak out so clearly against the Communist Party of China, it is important to know something of Chinese history in the 20th century. It was a terrible century for China. In the 1930s, until 1945, China was occupied by the Japanese army that treated the Chinese people brutally. Millions of Chinese were killed by the Japanese. In the late 1930s, Nanking was occupied and over 200,000 people were murdered. In 1945, civil war broke out again between the

1 **beyond a shadow of a doubt** [biˌɒnd ə ˈʃædəʊ əv ə ˈdaʊt] zweifellos • 3 **to affect** [əˈfekt] Auswirkungen haben auf • 4 **according to** [əˈkɔ:dɪŋ tu:] etw./jmdn. zufolge • 6 **muscle** [ˈmʌsl] Muskel • 7 **species** [ˈspi:ʃi:z] Spezies • 14 **to host** [həʊst] ausrichten • 14 **Olympics** [əʊˈlɪmpɪks] die Olympischen Spiele • 16 **union** [ˈju:njən] Gewerkschaft • 17 **standard** [ˈstændəd] Gesetze • 18 **to fulfil** [fʊlˈfɪl] erfüllen • 18 **obligation** [ˌɒblɪˈgeɪʃn] Verpflichtung • 26 **to occupy** [ˈɒkjəpaɪ] besetzen

Chinese Kuomintang Army supported by the US and Mao Tsetung's Chinese Communist People's Army. China was unified in 1949 by Mao.

He and the Chinese Communist Party gained power, and the Party is not ready to give it up. During the Cultural Revolution in the late 1960s and early 1970s, China was again in turmoil. Millions of people considered to be conservatives were killed or sent to the countryside to work on the fields. Only in the last 20 years has China slowly been opening. The reformer Deng Hsiaoping turned China towards capitalism. Today China has become a capitalist state with 8% growth per year – but the people do not have the personal freedom that people do in western democracies. In 1989 hundreds of thousands of Chinese people demonstrated for more personal freedom and for free elections. The People's Army was sent against them in Beijing. It is not known how many people were killed by the army in what became famous as the Tienanmen Massacre in 1989 (Tienanmen is the central square in Beijing).

The Communist Party is still in power and still determines what can be published, what people are allowed to say in public or what Chinese may say to foreigners and what not. For example, since China occupied Tibet in 1950, it is not allowed to speak of the "cultural genocide" of China against Tibet, as the Dalai Lama does. He is forced to live in India in exile.

But the picture is not simply black and white. There are many kinds of freedom in China today that were unthinkable even 15 years ago, for instance for writers or for film-makers. Chinese films are some of the most important films made today. Corrupt officials are often put on trial, but often not. The Internet has proven to be

3 **to unify** ['ju:nɪfaɪ] vereinigen • 4 **to gain power** [geɪn 'paʊə] an die Macht kommen • 7 **turmoil** ['tɜ:mɔɪl] Aufruhr, Unruhe • 8 **countryside** ['kʌntrɪsaɪd] *hier:* aufs Land • 12 **growth** [grəʊθ] Wachstumsrate • 20 **to determine** [dɪ'tɜ:mɪn] bestimmen • 21 **to publish** ['pʌblɪʃ] veröffentlichen • 30 **film-maker** ['fɪlm,meɪkə] Filmproduzent/-in • 31 **official** [ə'fɪʃl] Beamte/Beamtin

a real danger for the Communist Party, and many online dissidents (51 in 2008 alone, more than in any other country) were put in prison. In the same year, 2,500 web sites were blocked by the Party, according to *Reporteurs sans frontièrs*. An unknown number of dissidents are in prison. One of the most prominent and courageous people in China is a man named Hu Jia.

Hu was born in 1973 in Beijing and studied Information Technology there. In 1996 he finished his studies, and a year later he sacrificed a well-paid job with a Beijing TV channel to become an environmental activist. He worked for *Friends of Nature* and Hong Kong's *Friends of Earth*. He helped to teach Chinese farmers what would happen if they cut down their trees. A year later he protested against hunting the Tibetan antilope. Hu and his wife are both Buddhists and are against killing animals. In 1999 Hu discovered a blood scandal in the province Henan: to make some money, many Chinese donated blood – but the needles were HIV-positive, giving thousands of

10 **to sacrifice** ['sækrɪfaɪs] opfern • 15 **to hunt** [hʌnt] jagen • 18 **to donate** [dəʊ'neɪt] spenden • 19 **needle** ['ni:dl] Nadel

people AIDS. This was a big scandal in China. "I do not believe in taking life. This is why I helped the antelope and why I became an AIDS activist. I saw a family, a man and his wife and their child, and all of them died within two months of my seeing them. I feel life is so precious, but so easily taken away … ," he told the British newspaper *The Independent*.

Starting in 1999, Hu was arrested and threatened by the police again and again. In 2004, on the 15th anniversary of the Tienanmen Massacre, Hu put down yellow roses in Tienanmen Square in Peking. This was too much for the Communist Party because no one was allowed even to mention the Massacre. Like Aung San Suu Kyi in Burma, Hu was put under house arrest. In 2006 he was arrested again and disappeared for 41 days. Before that he had said that he would take part in a hunger strike in solidarity with other dissidents in prison. He was beaten by the police and was not given the medicine that he needed for the hepatitis-B that he had. After he was freed, he was put under house arrest without any legal reason.

During this time of being under house arrest, *The Independent* wrote about what happened when they visited him: "Going to see Mr Hu in his apartment complex … involved showing your press card at the police who ran alongside your car as you entered the compound. Then you had to pick your way around groups of police officers … smoking and chatting idly, or hassling Mr Hu's wife, Zeng Jinyan, as she left for work …."

The police occupied the apartments next to Hu's and Zeng's. In 2007, Hu's wife Zeng – an Internet activist for democracy – was also put under house arrest. When she was pregnant with their daughter, she had to get a permit

2 **to take life** [teɪk ˈlaɪf] töten • 4 **within** [wɪˈðɪn] innerhalb von • 5 **precious** [ˈpreʃəs] wertvoll • 8 **threaten** [ˈθretn] bedrohen • 9 **anniversary** [ˌænɪˈvɜːsri] Jahrestag • 24 **press card** [ˈpres kɑːd] Presseausweis • 25 **alongside** [əˌlɒŋˈsaɪd] neben • 27 **idly** [ˈaɪdli] müßig • 27 **to hassle** [ˈhæsl] schikanieren • 32 **pregnant** [ˈpregnənt] schwanger • 32 **permit** [ˈpɜːmɪt] Genehmigung

every time she wanted to leave the apartment to see a doctor.

Hu was arrested on 27th December, 2007, and sentenced to three and a half years in prison for “inciting to subvert state power” through several articles about freedom and for talking to foreign journalists – just four months before the Olympic Games began in Beijing.

By this time, Hu had become famous. The American TIME Magazine called him one of the “100 most influential people in the world today”. International human rights groups were outraged at the prison sentence. Amnesty International protested and said the Communist Party government was trying to warn any other activists “who dare to raise human rights concerns publicly”. His wife, said Hu, was beaten by the police. Amnesty International demanded his release immediately.

In the autumn of 2008, Hu was awarded the European Parliament’s top human rights award, the Sakharov Prize. The Chinese government was very angry that the European Parliament had showed solidarity with Hu in this way. “It is not only for us. It is also for all Chinese human rights defenders ,” Hu’s wife Zeng told the German Press Agency. Because Hu was in prison when he was to receive the award, a sign with his name was placed in front of an empty chair during the ceremony in Strasbourg. The European Parliament members all stood up and applauded. Hu said, “Perhaps the European Parliament was thinking of the work I did in the areas of AIDS and the environment, because what I did in terms of human rights was very far from sufficient and I will need to redouble my efforts.” Hu’s wife Zeng said that “sometimes the price to be paid is very, very high.”

4 **to incite** [ɪn'saɪt] anstiften • 4 **to subvert** [sʌb'vɜ:t] untergraben • 14 **to dare** [deə] wagen • 14 **concerns** [kən'sɜ:nz] *hier:* Themen • 22 **defender** [dɪ'fendə] *hier:* Verfechter/-in • 30 **sufficient** [sə'fɪʃnt] genug • 30 **to redouble** [ˌri:'dʌbl] verstärken • 31 **effort** ['efət] Bemühung

The price is very high for many other human rights activists in China, too. In 2008 human rights activists signed the "Charter 08", which demanded democracy and human rights. One of the most active people to sign was Liu Xiaobo who is now in prison. He received the Nobel Peace Prize in 2010.

Another activist is the artist Ai Weiwei, China's most famous living artist today. He was left alone by the Chinese secret police until 2009, when police broke into his apartment and beat him up because he called for freedom of speech and freedom of expression. Ai Weiwei is so famous, he thought the Chinese government would never dare to touch him. He was wrong. The police beating injured Ai's head so badly that he almost died later of a brain haemorrhage while he was in Munich for an exhibition of his art. German doctors saved his life.

There are many more like Hu Jia, Liu Xiaobo and Ai Weiwei who are willing to pay this price for the sake of freedom and human rights.

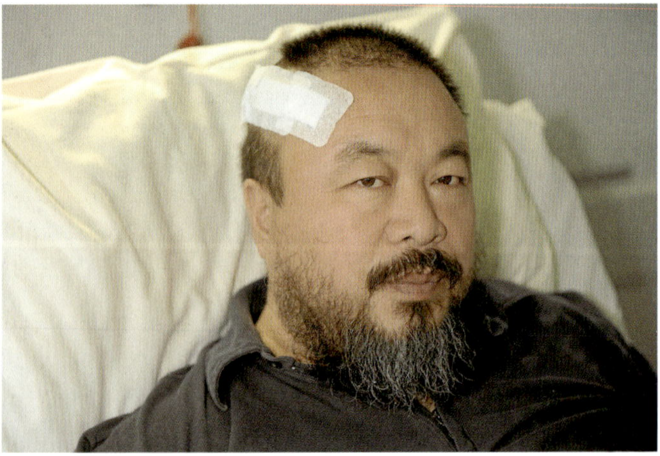

3 **charter** ['tʃɑ:tə] Charta • 11 **freedom of expression** [ˌfri:dəm əv ɪk'spreʃn] Freiheit der Meinungsäußerung • 13 **to touch sb** [tʌtʃ] *hier:* jmdn. etw. antun • 15 **brain haemorrhage** ['breɪn ˌhemrɪdʒ] Gehirnblutung • 18 **for the sake of** [ˌfə ðə 'seɪk əv] um einer Sache willen

# The death of Anna Politkovskaya

She did not notice the tall, dark-haired man standing in the corner of the downstairs hallway. She was a journalist and always in a hurry – this time, she had to finish a story by the next day. She did not notice the young woman who had followed her in the supermarket and who was filmed by the cameras there. She had parked her car, a small Lada, in front of the apartment building in Moscow where she lived. The car was full of groceries. She carried as much as she could upstairs, into the lift and into her apartment. Then she took the lift back down to fetch the rest of the groceries, and opened the lift doors downstairs.

It was the afternoon of 7th October, 2006.

Anna Politkovskaya (pronunciation: ˌpəlɪt'kɒfskəɪə) was born in 1958 in New York. She was the daughter of two Soviet diplomats who worked at the United Nations there. They belonged to the Soviet elite: anyone allowed to live in the West in those days was someone the Communist Party of the Soviet Union (1917-1991) could trust. As Politkovskaya said in an interview with the British *The Guardian newspaper* many years later: “I was a girl from a diplomatic family, a bit of a swot; I didn’t know life at all.” Politkovskaya studied journalism at Moscow State University and started to work for the national daily newspaper *Izvestia* in 1980. It was not easy being a journalist in a country with press censorship. Politkovskaya was very happy when in 1985 the new Soviet leader Mikhail Gorbachev began a new era of personal freedom and freedom of the press.

The Soviet Union called itself a socialist state under the dictatorship of the proletariat. In fact, it was non-capitalist planned economy state under the dictatorship of the Communist Party. Within the Communist Party, the

---

2 **hallway** ['hɔːlweɪ] Eingang(sbereich) • 8 **groceries** ['grəʊsrɪz] Lebensmittel • 10 **to fetch** [fetʃ] holen • 16 **elite** [ɪ'liːt] Elite • 18 **to trust** [trʌst] vertrauen • 21 **a bit** [bɪt] *hier:* etwas wie • 21 **swot** [swɒt] Streber/-in • 25 **censorship** ['sensəʃɪp] Zensur • 26 **era** ['ɪərə] Ära

Central Committee and very often one single man told everyone what to do – and what to think. In the 1980s the Soviet Union began to fall apart. Wrong reforms or no reforms at all, an economy that could not give its citizens many things they needed and, starting in 1979, a terrible war in Afghanistan that the Soviet Union was losing, a dramatic drop in the price of oil in 1985/86 – all this added up to a feeling of discontent in the Soviet Union. Many of the Soviet "republics" wanted to become independent from Moscow. A new era began with Gorbachev and the president that was next in the 1990s, Boris Yeltsin. These were golden years for Russian journalism, and for Anna Politkovskaya. At last, journalists had the freedom to write what they wanted to.

In his last years, Yeltsin often did not know what he was doing. A few times he appeared drunk on TV. Finally, he named his favourite, an intelligent young man, to become president. This young man was elected President of the Russian Federation in March, 2000. His name was Vladimir

1 **Central Committee** ['sentrl kə'mɪti] Zentralkomitee • 3 **to fall apart** [fɔ:l ə'pɑ:t] auseinanderbrechen • 7 **to add up to** [æd 'ʌp] führen zu • 8 **discontent** [ˌdɪskən'tent] Unzufriedenheit, Unmut • 17 **to name** [neɪm] *hier:* ernennen • 19 **Russian Federation** [rʌʃn ˌfedr'eɪʃn] Russische Föderation

Putin, and he had been the director of the Russian secret service, the Federal Security Service, the FSB. He was President until 2008.

The golden years for Russian journalists were over. Critical newspapers and TV and radio stations were closed down. Over the years, the official TV stations were forced to report more and more what President Putin wanted to hear. According to *Reporteurs sans frontièrs*, on a list for freedom of the press in 167 countries, Russia was at at number 140. Journalists were shot and it was never clear who had murdered them. The Russian parliament became an instrument of the President. Terrorist bombings in Moscow were used to introduce press censorship, at first for a few weeks, then for longer periods of time. Or as Anna Politkovskaya wrote, "All we have left is the Internet, where information is still freely available. For the rest, if you want to go on working as a journalist, it's total servility to Putin. Otherwise, it can be death, the bullet, poison, or trial – whatever our social services, Putin's guard dogs, see fit."

A few Russians became very, very rich after the year 2000, and many Russians became poorer. The life expectancy for men was 58 years. There was corruption everywhere in society, and the Russian Mafia shot anyone that got in their way. Russia was again a sick country. Journalists such as Anna Politkovskaya wanted to write about these facts – about corruption, about not having the freedom to write what they wanted, about the strange murders of writers and journalists, about the sick state of Russia. This became more and more difficult.

Since 1999 Politkovskaya worked for the pro-democracy newspaper *Novaya Gazeta* in Moscow. She was their special correspondent. Without ever wanting to do so, she became a war correspondent.

12 **bombing** ['bɒmɪŋ] Anschlag • 17 **servility** [sɜː'vɪləti] Unterwürfigkeit • 18 **otherwise** ['ʌðəwaɪz] sonst • 18 **bullet** ['bʊlɪt] Kugel • 18 **poison** ['pɔɪzn] Gift • 19 **to see fit** [siː 'fɪt] es für angebracht halten • 21 **life expectancy** [ˌlaɪf ɪk'spektnsi] Lebenserwartung • 23 **to get in the way** [ˌget ɪn ðə 'weɪ] im Wege stehen

In 1994 the Chechen Republic tried to become independent from Moscow. The Chechen soldiers knew the mountain area better than the Russian soldiers. President Yeltsin had to give up. In 1997 he signed a peace treaty giving Chechnya its independence. This was known as the First Chechen War. In 1999 war broke out again between Russia and Chechnya. Russia just did not want Chechnya to stay independent. The Russian offensive was better planned this time, and in February of 2000 Russia recaptured the Chechen capital of Grozny and most of the Chechen regions. There was terrible fighting for many years.

Politkovskaya was there and wrote critical reports about both sides – the brutalities of the Chechen soldiers and the brutalities of the Russian soldiers. She wrote about so-called ethnic cleansing by the Russians, about murders and rape and torture, repression and destroyed towns and about Grozny. It was completely destroyed by the Russians. Human rights violations became common, and Politkovskaya fearlessly wrote about them. She described murders, torture scenes and the horrible things that happened to the Chechen civilians. Once she was made prisoner by the Russian soldiers and was threatened with execution. For three days in 2001 she was kept in a hole in the ground without food or water. The same year she fled to Vienna because a Russian police officer who had committed atrocities against civilians wanted to kill her. He was arrested in 2002, set free, then put in prison in 2005 for torturing and murdering a Chechen civilian. Politkovskaya's article *Disappearing People* helped to put the man in prison. A day after she flew to Vienna, a neighbour of hers who looked a lot like Politkovskaya was

2 **Chechen Republic** [ˌtʃetʃ'en rɪ'pʌblɪk] Tschetschenische Republik • 4 **peace treaty** ['pi:s ˌtri:ti] Friedensvertrag • 10 **to recapture** [ˌri:'kæptʃə] zurückerobern • 16 **ethnic cleansing** [ˌeθnɪk 'klenzɪŋ] ethnische Säuberung • 17 **repression** [rɪ'preʃn] Unterdrückung • 19 **violation** [ˌvaɪə'leɪʃn] Verletzung • 22 **civilian** [sɪ'vɪliən] Zivilist/in • 24 **execution** [ˌeksɪ'kju:ʃn] Hinrichtung • 26 **to flee, fled, fled** [fli:] fliehen

shot in Moscow. But Politkovskaya could not stay away from her home and the war for very long. She returned to Russia, “If I don’t write any more, my enemies will have achieved their goal.”

In the year 2002 Chechen guerillas took hundreds of hostages in a Moscow musical theatre during a performance. Politkovskaya tried to help to reach an agreement between the two sides. But Russian special forces used poison gas in the theatre and killed all of the Chechen guerillas – and 129 hostages. Politkovskaya strongly criticized the way Russian special forces were used. She wrote that there had been no need to kill all the hostages.

In 2004 Chechen guerrillas again took hundreds of hostages in a school in the town Beslan in the north Caucasus. They were almost all school children. Politkovskaya again tried to help and on the flight to Chechnya she became terribly ill with what the media called food-poisoning. Politkovskaya was sure that she was poisoned during the flight. She survived.

Many people saw Politkovskaya as a human rights activist and not as a journalist. She was both, and more. She was a very courageous woman who managed to overcome her fear. “I have no hope left in my soul,” she told Britain’s *The Independent* newspaper. “Only a change of leadership would allow me to have hope, but it’s a political winter.” In her essay *Am I Afraid?* She wrote, “People often tell me that I am a pessimist, that I don’t believe in the strength of the Russian people, that I am obsessive in my opposition to Putin and see nothing beyond that. If anybody thinks they can take comfort from the ‘optimistic’ forecast, let

5 **guerrilla** [gə'rɪlə] Guerilla • 6 **hostage** ['hɒstɪdʒ] Geisel • 7 **to reach an agreement** [ˌri:tʃ ən ə'gri:mənt] eine Einigung erzielen • 19 **food-poisoning** ['fu:d ˌpɔɪznɪŋ] Lebensmittelvergiftung • 23 **to overcome** [ˌəʊvə'kʌm] überwinden • 28 **strength** [streŋkθ] Stärke • 29 **obsessive** [əb'sesɪv] besessen • 29 **opposition** [ˌɒpə'zɪʃn] Widerstand • 30 **beyond** [bɪ'ɒnd] weiter • 31 **to take comfort from** [teɪk 'kʌmpfət] sich trösten mit

them do so. It is certainly the easier way, but it is the death sentence for our grandchildren."

She also wrote, "People sometimes pay with their lives for saying aloud what they think. In fact, one can even get killed for giving me information. I am not the only one in danger."

She was not the only one, but she was in terrible danger and refused the offer of bodyguards. And so on that terrible day in October 2006 she opened the doors of the lift to fetch the rest of her groceries from her car. The tall man shot her four times and dropped the pistol in mafia style next to Politkovskaya's dead body.

There was international outrage at her death in Putin's Russia. The men accused of murdering her were set free in the first trial. It was a farce. Many people believe the murderers will never be caught.

Politkovskaya criticized the pro-Putin government in Chechnya and she criticized President Putin, the Russian army and the Chechen guerrillas, the Russian secret service and the special police OMON. They were all her enemies.

Between 2000 and 2006 13 other journalists were killed in Russia. One of the last was another courageous woman, Natalia Estemirova – in 2009, when Vladimir Putin was no longer president.

Anna Politkovskaya was one activist in the long line of Russian dissidents back in Soviet times: Andrei Sakharov and the great writer Alexander Solshenizyn, to name only two of them. In spite of the risk, the courageous protest continues.

---

1 **death sentence** ['deθ ˌsentəns] Todesurteil • 2 **grandchildren (pl.)** ['grændtʃɪldrn] Enkel • 8 **to refuse** [rɪ'fju:z] ablehnen • 14 **to set so free** [set 'fri:] jdn. freilassen

## Shirin Ebadi: "Our country doesn't need a hero."

The great Iranian human rights activist Shirin Ebadi (pronunciation: chɪ'ri:n ˌebɔ:'di) was born in northwestern Iran in 1947. "I spent my childhood in a family filled with kindness and affection," she wrote in 2003. Perhaps the love she felt in her family gave her the strength that she would need later in life. Ebadi came to Tehran with her family when she was one. She was a very intelligent girl and later studied law at Tehran University. In 1975 she was the first woman in Iranian history to become a judge. Then, in 1979, the Islamic Revolution changed the lives of millions. "I and other female judges were dismissed from our posts and given clerical duties. They made me a clerk in the very court I once presided over."

Before 1979, Iran was ruled by the "Shah", which is something like a king. The Shah was supported by the West, and he created lots of reforms that many religious people in Iran believed to be "western": women and men were equal, women were allowed to have the same jobs as men and to wear the clothes that they wanted to. People had lots of personal freedom – if they kept their mouths shut and did not criticize the corrupt regime. The bad side of the Shah's regime was that it was brutal. No opposition was allowed, political parties were banned, and tens of thousands of human rights activists were tortured and murdered by the Shah's terrible secret police, the SAVAK. Led by Ayatollah Khomeini, who still lived in exile in Paris, major demonstrations and strikes against the Shah's oppressive regime broke out in January of 1978.

1 **Iranian** [ɪ'reɪniən] iranisch • 4 **affection** [ə'fekʃn] Liebe, Zuneigung • 11 **female** ['fi:meɪl] weiblich • 12 **post** [pəʊst] Arbeitsplatz • 12 **clerical** ['klerɪkl] Büro- • 12 **clerk** [klɑ:k] *hier:* Gerichtsschreiber/-in • 13 **very** ['veri] genau • 13 **to preside** [prɪ'zaɪd] den Vorsitz haben • 27 **major** ['meɪdʒə] Groß-, Massen- • 28 **oppressive** [ə'presɪv] repressiv

In February of 1979, the Islamic Revolution overthrew the Shah of Iran. He fled the country.

Almost everyone in Iran was happy to get rid of the Shah, but in many ways life got worse for the Iranian people. Women were forced to give up of many jobs – such as being a judge, as Shirin Ebadi had been – and had to stop wearing make-up. They were forced to cover up and wear the chador in public. As before the Revolution in 1979, opposition was not allowed. Women had to obey their husbands.

Iran had become an Islamic state with very strict laws. This kind of Islam is called "fundamentalist", which means that the writings of the holy book, the Koran, are taken and applied as they are. There is no interpretation as with the Old or New Testament. What the Koran says is the law, or what the religious leader, the Ayatollah Khomeini, told the people. This kind of religious government is called "theocracy". On the day that he arrived back in Iran, on 1st February, 1979, Khomeini said about the regime of Bakhtiar, the prime minister at the time, "I shall kick their teeth in."

Many people's teeth were "kicked in" by the Islamic revolutionaries. Again, as under the Shah, thousands and thousands of human rights activists, workers, students, women, anyone who did not follow what the Ayatollah said, were put in prison, or tortured and murdered. The first to be executed were the members of the Shah's regime. The Iranian theocracy immediately became a regime with blood on its hands.

Fear was common in Iran. "Fear," Shirin Ebadi said, "like hunger, is an instinct. It comes whether you like it or not." When she lost her job as a judge, it took her years to get

8 **chador** [ˈtʃædə] Tschador (in islamischen Ländern von Frauen getragener Überwurf) • 9 **to obey** [əʊˈbeɪ] gehorchen • 13 **holy** [ˈhəʊli] heilig • 14 **to apply** [əˈplaɪ] *hier:* in der Praxis umsetzen • 18 **theocracy** [θiˈɒkrəsi] Theokratie, Gottesstaat • 20 **prime minister** [ˌpraɪm ˈmɪnɪstə] Premierminister

permission to practice as a lawyer. Finally, she received it and started to defend human rights activists and liberal people. Two of her clients, the liberal intellectuals Daryoush and his wife Parvaneh Forouhar, were stabbed to death in 1998 in a series of murders. The murderers were members of the Intelligence Ministry. In June of 2000, Ebadi was collecting material to prove that some of Iran's leaders, the mullahs, were behind the attacks on liberal people in Iran. She did not wait for the secret police to knock on her door. She was worried mostly about her family – she is married and has two adult children now – so she did not tell them where she was going. She turned herself in to the court and spent 23 days in prison. But because she was a devout Moslem, she was treated with respect by her guards.

She was later convicted of defaming the Islamic Republic and given a two-year suspended sentence. This did not stop her from defending mistreated children, oppressed women and political prisoners.

**1 permission** [pəˈmɪʃn] Erlaubnis, Genehmigung • **2 to defend** [dɪˈfend] verteidigen • **2 liberal** [ˈlɪbrl] *hier:* freiheitlich gesinnt • **4 to stab to death** [stæb] erstechen • **9 to knock** [nɒk] (an)klopfen • **13 devout** [dɪˈvaʊt] strenggläubig • **15 to convict** [kənˈvɪkt] für schuldig erklären • **15 to defame** [dɪˈfeɪm] diffamieren, verleumden • **16 suspended** [səˈspendɪd] *hier:* auf Bewährung • **17 oppressed** [əˈprest] unterdrückt

Ebadi had become famous. What might have saved her life is that she is a devout Moslem. She believes, however, that what the regime in Tehran does is wrong. She believes that Islam does not have to oppress people, especially women and children, and that Islam is compatible with democracy. "This is all because of a patriarchal culture that interprets Islam," she says. "I am out to fight this patriarchal culture." Many of the Islamic laws that oppress women, she believes, have no basis in Islam. These views on religion are not popular with many young people in Iran.

Many of the other things that Ebadi did were popular, though: in 1988 she wrote a book called *The Rights of the Child* – in a country where children's rights were unknown. In 1995 she was one of the founders of the Association for Support of Children's Rights. In 2001 she founded the Human Rights Defence Centre. All the time, she defended liberal journalists and children that were mistreated or killed. Thanks to Ebadi, a law was debated and ratified in 2002 prohibiting all forms of violence against children. Ebadi also gave talks in many cities in Iran and spoke out for the rights of the individual. Once she was giving a speech at the all-women Al Zahra University in Tehran, and 50 bearded thugs ran towards her and shouted "Death to Ebadi!". Quickly, students surrounded Ebadi and helped her down the stairs, where she was saved by the police. She had become Iran's most important human rights activist.

In 2003, she was the first Moslem woman and the first Iranian to receive the Nobel Peace Prize. "The prize proves the path I have taken is the right one," she said quietly. "It shows people that struggling for human rights is the right thing to do." The prize was given to her for her efforts

5 **compatible** [kəm'pætɪbl] vereinbar • 6 **patriarchal** [ˌpeɪtri'ɑ:kl] patriarchalisch • 15 **association** [əˌsəʊʃi'eɪʃn] Vereinigung • 19 **to ratify** ['rætɪfaɪ] unterzeichnen • 20 **to prohibit** [prəʊ'hɪbɪt] verbieten, untersagen • 24 **bearded** ['bɪədɪd] bärtig • 24 **thug** [θʌg] Rowdy • 25 **to surround** [sə'raʊnd] umringen • 26 **stairs** [steəz] Treppe

for democracy and human rights, especially for the rights of children and of women. The regime in Tehran was not happy that Ebadi had received the prize.

In 2008 Ebadi told Reuters news agency that Iran's human rights record had gotten worse. In April 2008 she said, "Threats against my life and security and those of my family, which began some time ago, have intensified." Human Rights Watch said they were "extremely worried" about Ebadi's safety.

In the summer of 2009 there were widespread demonstrations in many Iranian cities, especially in Tehran, for human rights and against the regime of the mullahs. Ebadi told the international press that she was against economic sanctions because they only hurt the people; but she called for political sanctions against the government.

Ebadi is sure that the young people in Iran will stay political, even though they have lost the battle of 2009. Thousands were thrown into prison and mistreated, many were murdered. Ebadi will continue to defend the rights of the individual, and of political prisoners in court.

She has not lost hope.

## Dominik Brunner, German hero

Many "heroes" are not famous and do not receive any awards. No reporters ever come to interview them. Only their friends, family and colleagues know about them. There is nothing spectacular about their lives. They work hard and perhaps decide to do something good, or something dangerous, and then take the bus home the

6 **threat** [θret] Drohung • 6 **security** [sɪ'kjʊərəti] Sicherheit • 7 **to intensify** [ɪn'tensɪfaɪ] verschärfen • 14 **economic sanctions** [ˌi:kə'nɒmɪk 'sæŋkʃn] Wirtschaftssanktionen • 25 **colleague** ['kɒli:g] Kollege/Kollegin • 26 **spectacular** [spek'tækjələ] Besonderes

same night and watch the news on TV. They do not appear in the news, though. They are the people next door.

Dominik Brunner was one such man, the man next door. He was born in 1959 in Lower Bavaria and grew up in Ergoldsbach. He studied Law in Munich and was employed at the same firm that his father was, too, a Bavarian company that produces roofing tiles. In 1994 Dominik Brunner was promoted to the top management of his firm. He dealt with finances, organization, personnel, procuring and legal questions. He was a busy man, but – as head of personnel – he made it his business to help his colleagues. Brunner always had time for a friendly chat and he was considered a good person. He was greatly respected in his firm, and his friends and colleagues all agreed: this is a decent man.

In the spring of 2009 Brunner moved back to Ergoldsbach, very near the house of his elderly parents who needed his help. He still kept a city apartment in Munich and commuted from Ergoldsbach to Munich. On 12th September, 2009, Brunner took the S-Bahn from Munich central station. At the station Donnersbergerbrücke four children got on the same train that Brunner was on. They were followed by two German youths, the 17- and 18-year-olds Markus and Sebastian, who had tried to get

7 **roofing tiles** ['ru:fɪŋ taɪl] Dachziegel • 8 **to be promoted** [prə'məʊtɪd] befördert werden • 10 **procuring** [prə'kjʊəɪŋ] Beschaffung(swesen) • 15 **decent** ['di:snt] anständig • 23 **to commute** [kə'mju:t] pendeln • 27 **central** ['sentrl] Haupt-

money from the children earlier. The children refused to give them the money. The youths made threatening comments to them while they were all still on the S-Bahn. Brunner became involved in order to protect the children. When the youths kept making comments, Brunner called the police on his mobile and asked them to meet him at the Munich-Solln S-Bahn station. The police promised to be there soon.

When Brunner and the four children got off the S-Bahn at Solln, Markus and Sebastian got off as well. Brunner stood in front of the children to protect them. The situation, first a verbal exchange, then became physical. Brunner tried to defend the four children and himself by hitting one of the youths. Then the two youths attacked Brunner. One of the youths had even stuck a key between his fingers to hit Brunner with his key and his fist. Brunner went down and could not defend himself any more. The two youths kept on attacking for a time even after Brunner was lying on the platform. He had 22 wounds. People had called to the attackers to leave Brunner in peace; many people rang the police. One man tried to get to Brunner from the other side of the S-Bahn tracks, but had to hurry back when an S-Bahn entered the Solln station. A man, a pupil from a Gymnasium and a doctor's assistant gave Brunner first aid.

Shortly after, the police cars started arriving. The two attackers had hidden themselves behind some bushes to see what was going to happen. People who were there pointed them out to the police and they were immediately arrested. Dominik Brunner died on the way to the hospital. He was 50 years old. His attackers were charged with murder and manslaughter.

12 **verbal exchange** [ˌvɜːbl ɪksˈtʃeɪndʒ] Wortwechsel • 15 **to stick, stuck, stuck** [stɪk, stʌk, stʌk] stecken • 15 **key** [kiː] Schlüssel • 16 **fist** [fɪst] Faust • 19 **wound** [wuːnd] Wunde • 24 **first aid** [fɜːst ˈeɪd] erste Hilfe • 31 **to charge with sth** [tʃɑːdʒ] jdn. wegen etw. anklagen • 32 **manslaughter** [ˈmænslɔːtə] Totschlag

The brutality of the murder surprised and shocked anyone who heard about it; it was in the news many days after 12th September. Almost two weeks after the murder there were three large demonstrations of solidarity with Dominik Brunner.

The funeral service was very moving. The Bavarian Minister President awarded Brunner the Bavarian "Verdienstorden", and Federal President Horst Köhler gave the "Bundesverdienstkreuz" to Brunner's parents, the highest award that Germany has, for the outstanding courage their son had shown.

Brunner's death sparked a big discussion in Germany – about teenage crime, about the teenage criminal code, and about the courage to stand up for what one believes is right. There has also been a lot of discussion about how Brunner handled the situation, and why some aspects about the case only later became public. It only came out later, for example, that Brunner died not directly because of the 22 wounds, but because of an enlarged heart muscle that failed as a result of the traumatic situation (cardiac failure).

It is easy to take sides in a controversial discussion such as this, but one must first know the facts. For one, teenage crime has decreased over the last decades. For another, the teenage criminal code is not ineffective. It can be just as hard on the criminal as the adult criminal code can be. But these questions are the most difficult and the most important to answer: Should you or should you not stand up for your beliefs, even when it is dangerous to do so, and how do you best do this?

These are the central questions of this book.

6 **funeral service** ['fju:nrl 'sɜ:vɪs] Beerdigung • 10 **outstanding** [ˌaʊt'stædɪŋ] außergewöhnlich • 13 **teenage crime** ['ti:neɪdʒ kraɪm] Jugendkriminalität • 13 **teenage criminal code** ['ti:neɪdʒ ˌkrɪmɪnl kəʊd] Jugendstrafgesetz • 17 **case** [keɪs] Fall • 19 **enlarged** [ɪn'lɑ:dʒd] vergrößert • 20 **cardiac failure** [ˌkɑ:diæk 'feɪljə] Herzversagen • 24 **to decrease** [dɪ'kri:s] sinken • 28 **to stand up for** [stænd 'ʌp] sich einsezten für

Many people in Germany may stand up for what is right every day, but we rarely learn of this because nothing bad happens to them. Dominik Brunner's case was the exception, crime specialists say, and that is why it made the headlines: *because* it was unusual and *because* it ended in a tragedy. "What one shouldn't do," Kai Jonas, social psychologist from the University of Amsterdam said, "is to play the lonely hero. It is better to lead the victim away from the attacker, to break up the magnetic field between victim and criminal, for instance by pretending that I know the victim and haven't seen the person in a long time. One should think how one could de-escalate the conflict. Acting the right way can minimize a conflict." Jonas was then asked if Brunner had acted incorrectly. He answered, "... He (Brunner) was obviously a very courageous man who acted without realizing the consequences. But that's the way it is if you stand up for your beliefs. Many that act courageously don't think over all possible consequences , or they ignore the dangers for themselves. I can't criticize Herr Brunner posthumously."

Perhaps Dominik Brunner did not handle the situation in the best way possible, but this is easily said in retrospect. He acted in the way he thought best at the time, with the motivation to protect those who were weaker than he was. Dominik Brunner ended up giving his life when he did the right thing.

4 **exeption** [ɪk'sepʃn] Ausnahme • 4 **crime specialist** [kraɪm 'speʃlɪst] Kriminologe/Kriminologin • 8 **victim** ['vɪktɪm] Opfer • 12 **to de-escalate** [ˌdiː'eskleɪt] deeskalieren, entschärfen • 13 **to act** [ækt] handeln • 16 **consequence** ['kɒnsɪkwəns] Folge • 20 **posthumously** ['pɒstjəməsli] nach dem Tod • 22 **in retrospect** [ɪn 'retrəspekt] im Nachhinein

## Reading help

These ideas can help you to read even better – not only the texts in this book, but any text. You can follow these six steps, or do only some of them.

**Step 1 Pre-reading activities**

- First look at the title of the text and the picture(s).
- Think what the text could be about.
- Start a mind map for words you think will be used in the text.

**Step 2 While-reading activities**

- Stop reading when you want to and think what may happen next, and what the ending could be.
- Do not worry about being wrong. Think out loud!

**Step 3 Reading**

- Read the text once. This is "skimming". Find out what the text is about.
- In this book: Look at the new words at the bottom of the page or at the human rights vocabulary on page 4.
- Second reading: Scan the text and look for a keyword in each paragraph. You can underline or highlight them.

**Step 4 Post-reading**

- Note-taking: Make notes about each paragraph. Your written notes should be short, so you can use these things: grids or mind maps or symbols.
- You can also imagine the story as if it were a film.

**Step 5 Summarizing**

- Using your notes, summarize the whole text in a few sentences. – Summarizing shows that you have understood the text.
- Then summarize the text in just one sentence.

**Step 6 Answering questions and discussing a text**

- If the text is still difficult for you, answer all the questions given in this book, or work with a partner and ask and answer each other questions about the text.
- Then discuss the text in a group or in class. Think about this: What could the text be trying to tell the reader? Do you agree with the way the protagonist is acting? Do you agree with the author? Always give reasons for your answers.

There are many more points for discussion in this book.

## Exercises

### 1 Gandhi's long Salt March

a) 1. Why was 12th March, 1930, the beginning of the end of the British Empire in India?
   2. What is 'Satyagraha'?
   3. Why did the Indian people admire Gandhi?
   4. Gandhi once said "An eye for an eye, and soon the whole world is blind." What do you think this means?

b) *Think about this: Why was Gandhi so important for the 20th century?*

### 2 Raoul Wallenberg

a) *Make a mind map with the words needed to explain what Wallenberg did in Budapest in 1944. Put the words "Wallenberg's rescue operation" at the centre.*

b) *Use the mind map to describe in your own words what Wallenberg did in 1944.*

## 3 Gandhi and Wallenberg

a) *Gandhi's and Wallenberg's methods were different. Say what the differences are.*

b) *Think about this: Why were their methods different?*

## 4 Rosa Parks

a) *Why did Rosa Parks stay seated?*

b) *Why was her act of civil disobedience so important for the civil rights movement in the US?*

## 5 Nelson Mandela

a) *Say what Apartheid was.*

b) *Characterize Nelson Mandela. Start:* 'Rolihlahla' means 'troublemaker', and Mandela …

c) *Think about this: What do you think made Mandela a great man?*

## 6 Aung San Suu Kyi

a) *Match the sentence parts:*

| | |
|---|---|
| The Golden Triangle provides | Burma, The Jewel of Asia. |
| "Mynamar" was once called | Gandhi's Satyagraha. |
| The Burmese "junta" means | a mob while travelling. |
| Suu Kyi soon became | Generals with political power. |
| She was attacked by | the Burmese voice of freedom. |
| Suu Kyi believes in | opium for the world markets. |

b) *What do you think of Suu Kyi?*

## 7 Ken Saro-Wiwa

a) *Why was Saro-Wiwa against the oil industry?*

b) *What do the Nigerian and Burmese generals have in common?*

## 8 Julia 'Butterfly' Hill

a) *List the things that happened in Julia Hill's life that made her an environmental activist.*

b) *What was her idea of love and why was it so important for her?*

c) 1. What was unusual about her methods?
2. Do you agree with her methods?

## 9 Hu Jia

a) *Look at the text and make a list of the things you know about the Communist Party of China.*

b) *Use your list and think about this: Why is the Communist Party of China afraid of civil rights activists such as Hu Jia?*

## 10 Anna Politkovskaya

*Underline the two most emotional sentences in this chapter and give reasons for your choice.*

## 11 Hu Jia and Anna Politkovskaya

a) *Say what their struggle for human rights has in common, and what the differences are.*

b) *Say why they are very courageous people.*

## 12 Shirin Ebadi

a) *How are Ebadi's methods completely different from Politkovskaya's and Julia Hill's?*

b) *Ebadi says: "Our country doesn't need a hero." Discuss the pros and cons of this statement.*

c) *Discuss: Ebadi believes that the "patriarchal culture that interprets Islam" is at fault for the oppression of human rights in Iran and in Arab states.*

## 13 Dominik Brunner

a) *Why was Dominik Brunner "the man next door"?*

b) *What aspects are unusual about the Dominik Brunner case?*

c) *Discussion: How far should you go to stand up for your beliefs?*

d) *Think of a threatening situation that you might experience (or perhaps have experienced). What steps could you take to de-escalate this situation?*

## 14 General points for discussion

a) *Do you admire any of the people in this book especially? Give reasons. If not, give reasons.*

b) *Look back at your answers "Before you read this book" on page 3. Do you still agree with your ideas?*

c) *Think about who the author of this book considers a "true hero". Do you agree with the term "true hero" and what he considers to be a hero?*

d) *If you do not agree with the term, find another term.*

e) *Some human rights activists were able to change more than other activists. Compare cases where they were able to succeed, and where not. Why do you think they were sometimes successful, and sometimes not?*

## 15 Human rights project

There are many, many more human rights activists and organizations in the 20th and 21st century.

*Research one or more of them. Here are a few ideas:*

Mukhtaran Mai from Pakistan • Wangari Maathai from Kenya • Roberto Saviano from Italy

German resistance heroes: Hans and Sophie Scholl • the Kreisauer Kreis • Claus Schenk Graf von Stauffenberg • Georg Elser

The résistance in France: Jean Moulin

Organizations: Human Rights Watch • amnesty international • Greenpeace • Robin Wood • Reporteurs sans frontièrs

Step 1: Research the person/organization in a group.
Step 2: Present your group findings in a talk or: Gallery walk: each group makes a poster of their character/organization.
Step 3: Hang up the posters. The class does a "gallery walk" and looks at all the posters.
Step 4: Discuss in class which poster is the most convincing.
Step 5: Discuss why each group picked this character/organization, and why he/she or it is important for each group.

# Solutions

## Before you read this book

Individuelle Schülerantworten

## Exercises

**1 Gandhi's long Salt March**

a) 1. Gandhi's Salt March was an act of civil disobedience that broke the moral power of the British Empire. 2. Satyagraha is peaceful resistance. 3. Gandhi was a very courageous man whose civil disobedience achieved moral victories. 4. Gandhi believed that violence leads to even more violence.

b) Through his actions Gandhi showed everyone that Satyagraha could achieve victory, and that everyone could take part in civil disobedience if necessary.

**2 Raoul Wallenberg**

a) –

b) Wallenberg saved tens of thousands of Jews from death. He was able to create Swedish zones of safety, he gave Jews Swedish passports and he was even able to trick one of the worst Nazis, Adolf Eichmann.

**3 Gandhi and Wallenberg**

a) Gandhi used civil resistance against the British government. It took many years, but his method ended British colonialism. Wallenberg's method was much more active and even more dangerous than Gandhi's methods.

b) Their methods were different for two reasons: British colonialism was terrible, but not as terrible as the Nazi occupation of Europe and the murder of six million Jews. The other reason was that Gandhi had much more time than Wallenberg to achieve his goals, but Wallenberg had to act very quickly to keep the Budapest Jews out of the Nazi concentration camps.

**4 Rosa Parks**

a) Rosa Parks stayed seated because she was tired of giving in.

b) Rosa Parks's act of civil disobedience showed that she refused to accept segregation.

**5 Nelson Mandela**

a) Apartheid separated blacks from whites in all situations. It also meant that the racist Apartheid regime oppressed the black majority.
b) … was very intelligent and did not want to accept Apartheid.
c) Individuelle Schülerantworten

**6 Aung San Suu Kyi**

a) The Golden triangle … opium for…; "Myanmar" was … Burma, The Jewel …; The Burmese junta … Generals with …; Suu Kyi soon became … the Burmese voice …; She was attacked by … a mob while …; Suu Kyi believes in … Gandhi's Satyagraha.
b) Individuelle Schülerantworten

**7 Ken Saro-Wiwa**

a) He was against the oil industry because it destroyed Ogoniland and put money in the pockets of corrupt dictators.
b) They didn't care about human rights and they were all corrupt.

**8 Julia 'Butterfly' Hill**

a) List: butterfly landed on her when she was a little girl, terrible car accident, tree-sit, redwoods being destroyed
b) Her idea about love was that it should be active. It also meant that she would only use civil disobedience, not violence.
c) 1. Unusual: climbing a tree and living with it for a long time.
2. Individuelle Schülerantworten

**9 Hu Jia**

a) List: victory in civil war 1949, led by Mao Tse-tung, occupation of Tibet in 1950 and "cultural genocide" (Dalai Lama) of Tibet, 1989 massacre of people at Tienanmen in Beijing, still in power today, but things are slowly changing
b) Because people like Hu Jia show the people that they are not free yet. Hu Jia points to what is wrong in China.

**10 Anna Politkovskaya**

Individuelle Schülerantworten

**11 Hu Jia and Anna Politkovskaya**

a) In common: Both of them sacrificed their personal safety because they told the truth about their government. Differences:

Hu at first was an environmental and AIDS activist, Politkovskaja was a journalist who wrote critical articles.
b) They risked prison and even death.

**12 Shirin Ebadi**
a) Ebadi studied law and was a lawyer and judge. She worked more "within the system" than Politkovskaja or Hill.
b) + c) Individuelle Schülerantworten.

**13 Dominik Brunner**
a) There was nothing spectacular about his life.
b) Suddenly in his life, he realized that he must become active and protect some children. For him, phoning the police wasn't enough.
c) + d) Individuelle Schülerantworten

**14 General points for discussion**
Individuelle Schülerantworten

**15 Human rights project**
Individuelle Schülerantworten

## Pronunciation: a selection of names and places

### Introduction
Abraham Lincoln [ˌeɪbrəhæm 'lɪŋkən]
Alexander the Great [ˌælɪg'zɑ:ndə ðə 'greɪt]
Caesar ['sɪzə]
Napoleon [nə'pəʊliən]
George Washington [dʒɔ:dʒ 'wɒʃɪŋtən]
Dwight D. Eisenhower [dwaɪt di: 'eɪzənhaʊə]
Douglas MacArthur [ˌdʌglɪs mək'ɑ:θə]

### Gandhi
Ahmedabad [ɑ:'medəbɑ:d]
Dharasana [ˌdʌrɑ:'sɑ:nə]
Mohandas Gandhi [məˌhændəs 'gændi]
Porbandar [ˌpɔ:rə'bændʌ]
Durban ['dɜ:bən]
Mahatma [mə'hætmə]

### Raoul Wallenberg
Per Anger [peɪ 'ʌŋə]
Albert Einstein [ˌælbət 'aɪnstaɪn]
Sir Winston Churchill [sɜ: ˌwɪnstən 'tʃɜ:tʃɪl]

### Rosa Parks
Montgomery [mən'gʌmri]
Alabama [ˌælə'bæmə]
Detroit [də'trɔɪt]
Michigan ['mɪʃɪgən]
Dr Martin Luther King, Jr. [ˌmɑ:tɪn ˌlu:θə 'kɪŋ ˌdʒu:niə]

### Nelson Mandela
Transkei [ˌtrænt'skaɪ]
Johannesburg [dʒəʊ'hænɪsbɜ:g]
Frederick Willem de Klerk [ˌvɪləm də 'kleək]
Transvaal ['trænzvɑ:l]
Sharpeville Massacre ['ʃɑ:pvɪl]
Umkhonto we Sizwe [ʊm'kɒntɒ we 'sɪzwə]
Robben Island [ˌrɒbn 'aɪlənd]
Cape Town ['keɪptaʊn]

### Aung San Suu Kyi
Burma ['bɜ:mə]
Myanmar ['mjænmɑ:]
Mandalay [ˌmændəl'eɪ]
Bhutan [bu:'tɑ:n]
Depayin [de'pɑ:jɪn]

### Ken Saro-Wiwa
Ogoni [ə'gəʊni]
Nigeria [naɪ'dʒɪəriə]
Niger Delta ['naɪdʒə ˌdeltə]
Sani Abacha [ə'bætʃə]
British Petroleum [ˌbrɪtɪʃ pə'trəʊliəm]

### Julia Hill
Pennsylvania [ˌpensɪl'veɪniə]
MAXXAM ['mæksəm]
Sequoia National Park [sɪ'kwɔɪə]

Fayetteville [ˈfeɪetvɪl]
Quito [ˈkiːtəʊ]
Occidental Petroleum [ˌɒksɪˈdentl pəˈtrəʊliəm]

## Hu Jia

Kuomintang Army [ˌkwəʊmɪnˈtʌŋ ˌɑːmi]
Mao Tse-tung [ˌmaʊtseɪˈtʊŋ]
Tiananmen [tiˌænənˈmɪn]
Hongkong [ˌhɒŋˈkɒŋ]
Henan [hɔˈnʌn]
Zeng Jinyan [zeŋ dʒɪnˈiːæn]
Liu Xiaobo [ˌljuː ʃʌˈbɒ]
Ai Weiwei [aɪ weɪˈweɪ]

## Anna Politkovskaya

Soviet Union [ˌsəʊviət ˈjuːnjən]
Izvestia [ɪzˈvestɪə]
Novaya Gazeta [ˌnɒvəjə gəˈzetə]
Vienna [viˈenə]
Natalia Estemirova [nəˈtælɪə ˌestəˈmɪrəʊvə]
Alexander Solshenizyn [ˌælɪksˈɑːndə ˌsɒltʃəˈnɪtsn]

## Shirin Ebadi

Ayatollah Khomeini [ˌaɪəˈtɒlə ˌchɒməˈni]
Bakhtiar [ˌbʌchtɪˈɑːr]
Daryoush Forouhar [ˌdʌrɪˈuːʃ fruːˈhɑːr]
Parvaneh Forouhar [ˌpʌrvʌˈne fruːˈhɑːr]